14-C
12-96

P9-BZG-898

√ √ √ √ JAN √ 1994

332.678 PER
Perritt, Gerald W.
Diversify your way to wealth

Addison Public Library
235 N. Kennedy Drive
Addison, IL 60101
Phone: 708-543-3617

GAYLORD

DIVERSIFY
your way to
WEALTH

How to Customize Your
Investment Portfolio to Protect
and Build Your Net Worth

REVISED EDITION

Gerald W. **Perritt** & Alan **Lavine**

PROBUS PUBLISHING COMPANY
Chicago, Illinois
Cambridge, England

© 1994, Gerald W. Perritt and Alan Lavine

ALL RIGHTS RESERVED. No part of this publication may be reproduced, stored in a retrieval system, or transmitted, in any form or by any means, electronic, mechanical, photocopying, recording, or otherwise, without the prior written permission of the publisher and the copyright holder.

This publication is designed to provide accurate and authoritative information in regard to the subject matter covered. It is sold with the understanding that the author and the publisher are not engaged in rendering legal, accounting, or other professional service.

Authorization to photocopy items for internal or personal use, or the internal or personal use of specific clients, is granted by PROBUS PUBLISHING COMPANY, provided that the U.S. $7.00 per page fee is paid directly to Copyright Clearance Center, 222 Rosewood Drive, Danvers, MA 01923, USA; Phone: 1-508-750-8400. For those organizations that have been granted a photocopy license by CCC, a separate system of payment has been arranged. The fee code for users of the Transactional Reporting Service is 1-55738-546-7/94/$00.00 + $7.00.

ISBN 1-55738-546-7

First Edition © 1990, Longman Financial Services Publishing, a division of Longman Financial Services Institute, Inc.

Printed in the United States of America

BB

1 2 3 4 5 6 7 8 9 0

Probus books are available at quantity discounts when purchased for business, educational, or sales promotional use. For more information, please call the Director, Corporate / Institutional Sales at (800) 998-4644, or write:

Director, Corporate / Institutional Sales
Probus Publishing Company
1925 N. Clybourn Avenue
Chicago, IL 60614
FAX (312) 868-6250   PHONE (800) 998-4644

Dedication

To Gail and Gail, our lovely wives

CONTENTS

Preface   xv

Acknowledgments   xix

PART I   Why Diversify?   1

Chapter 1   What Is Asset Allocation?   3

Don't Bet the Ranch on a Single Hand: Diversification Reduces Risk • Baby Boomers Got Burned • You Must Consider the Risks • Corporate Profits Important • Inflation • Price Volatility • Hold a Lot of Different Investments • Protection through Diversification • Hedging Your Bets • The High Price of Togetherness • High Return with Lower Risk • Investing to Win, Place and Show

Chapter 2   What Is Your Level of Risk?   21

Zeroing In on Your Financial Needs and Goals • Pay Yourself First • Accumulate Money • Finding Money to Invest • How Much Are You Worth? • Cut the Fat Out of the Family Budget • Reclaim Wasteful Spending • Compare Last Year's Expenses to This Year's • Where to Cut Spending • Managing Your Cash as a Corporate Treasurer Would • How Much Will Your Money Be Worth? • The Investment Risks • The

Insomnia Factor • How Much Are You Willing to Lose? • What Investments Are Right for You? • How Risky Is Risky? • How Investments Stack Up • Creating an Investment Mix: Getting the Best Return with the Least Amount of Risk • Your Comfort Level

**Chapter 3 How to Split Up
         Your Investment Pie   39**
Combining Assets • Risk Averse • Your Financial Passages • How You Split It Up • Ladder Your Maturities • Watch the Yield Curve for Clues • What to Do Now • An Inflation Antidote • The Real Estate Question • REITs • Mutual Funds Think for You • A Financial Boilermaker • The Stock-Bond Seesaw • Safety in Treasury Bonds • Investing Overseas • A Wider Investment Choice • Top Performers Overseas • No Pain, No Gain • Foreign Bonds • Still No Free Lunch • Mix and Match

PART 2 Building Your Portfolio   59

Chapter 4 Individual Securities   61
Take a Long-Term Approach • Is the Stock Market Rigged? • One Step Back, Then Two Steps Forward • Stocks Beat T-Bills Hands Down • The Longer You Hold Stocks, the Less You May Lose • Over the Short Term You Can Pick Up Bigger Gains • The Longer You Hold Stocks, the More You Outperform T-Bills • The Longer the Holding Period, the Lower the Annual Loss • The More You Invest a Year, the Bigger Your Gain • Back to Basics • You're an Owner in the Company When You

Buy Stock • Long-Term Gains and Short-Term Swings • Do Your Homework • Is a Stock Undervalued or Overvalued? • Assess the Firm's Financial Strength • How to Pick Growth Stocks • What Is a Growth Firm? • Stages of Corporate Growth • When to Invest • What Should You Pay for Growth Stock? • Balancing Your Growth-Stock Portfolio • It Pays to Keep Your Balance • Best Approach • Diversify Your Stock Portfolio • Blue-Chip Stock Values • Dividends Are Important, Too • Reinvesting Dividends Boosts Returns • Dividends Are More Stable • Cash Cows • Gold-Mining Stocks and Bullion • Gold Stocks • Selecting Mining Stocks • Investing in the Metal • How to Buy Gold • Overseas Stocks • Closed-End Overseas Stock Funds • ADRs • Bond Basics • Understanding Bond Yields • Fixed-Income Risk • Reducing Interest-Rate Risk • Reducing Credit Risk • Treasury Bonds Avoid Credit Risk • A Word About Inflation and Stock Prices: Public Enemy Number One • We Have to Live with Some Inflation • When Bond Fund Investors Win • When Stock Fund Investors Win

Chapter 5 Mutual Funds   109
Funds Diversify for You • Pay Yourself Instead of Your Broker • Stalking the Wild No-Load Fund • Other Advantages • Long-Term Performance • Wide Price Swings Pay Off • Types of Mutual Funds • The Best Funds for Your Portfolio • Narrowing the Field • Count Your Mutual Funds • How Many Funds? • Strategies • Don't Buy Everything

Chapter 6   Model Mutual-Funds Portfolios   133
Mutual-Funds Front-Runners • Aggressive
Portfolio Mix • Moderately Aggressive Mix •
Growth and Income Mix • Income Mix • All-
Weather Portfolios • Generic Asset-Allocation
Portfolio • Low-Risk Asset-Allocation Portfo-
lio • Moderate-Risk Asset-Allocation Portfolio
• Higher-Risk Capital-Appreciation Allocation
Portfolio • Fund Profiles • Don't Rule Out
Other No-Load Funds

Chapter 7   How to Evaluate Performance   143
The Secret of Value-Added Gain • Quick and
Easy Way • A Word About All-In-One Funds
• Do Some Undercover Work • Keep Abreast
of Your Budget and Investments

PART 3   Asset-Allocation Strategies   157

Chapter 8   Dollar Cost Averaging   159
It's Not Scintillating • A Proven Commodity • A Few Strings

Chapter 9   Formula Investing   169
You Cannot Beat a Bull Market • Investing
for Uncertain Times • Rules for Timing
Buying and Selling • Constant-Dollar Plan
• It's Easy to Do • Matching Your Comfort
Level • Banking Profits • No Sure-Fire
Winners • Constant-Ratio Investing • A
Practicum • Profit-Taking Plus Dollar Cost
Averaging • Rebalancing Your Diversified
Portfolio • How It Works • Safety Is the
Key • Rebalance Based on Your Risk Level

**Chapter 10   Market Timing versus
            Buy-And-Hold Strategies   185**

Avoid Market Timing • Successful Coin Flip-
pers • Hot Over the Short Run • You Can-
not Beat the Average Over the Long Haul •
And When You're Not You're Not • Catch the
Turns by Staying Fully Invested • Easy Way
to Invest and Profit • Get Amnesia • If You
Can't Beat 'Em, Join 'Em • Being Right Part
of the Time Does Not Beat the Market •
Bear Scares • Diversify • 5 Best And 5
Worst Periods in the Market

Chapter 11   Retirement Savings Plans   201

Pot of Gold at the End of the Rainbow • Tax-
Deferred Growth • How Long Your Money
Will Last • Income Based on Life Expectancy
• Retirement Plans: Tax-Free Savings • IRA
Rules • Salary-Reduction Plans • Flexible
Plans • Traditional Pension Plans and Retire-
ment Savings • Defined Benefits When You
Retire • Or You Can Make Predetermined
Contributions • Life-Insurance Products Cost
Too Much • Term Insurance Covers Basic
Needs • Whole Life • Universal Life • Vari-
able Life • Single-Premium Life • Too Many
Fees • Raw Deal When You Borrow • A
Question to Ask Before You Buy

**Chapter 12   The Changing World
            of Mutual Funds   215**

Another Brokerage Firm Rip-Off • Some Call
Themselves Financial Planners • Best Deal:
No Transaction Fees Accounts • How It
Works • Variable Annuities • Investment
Options • High Fees—So Shop Around •

The Best Deals • Shopping for a Financial
Planner • How to Find a Good Financial
Planner • Conclusion

Conclusion   **225**
Diversify! Diversify! Diversify! • You Can't
Plead Insanity for a Parking Ticket • All
Great Bull Markets End • Get in a Good
Position Now • Select Top No-Load Mutual-
Fund Families • Do Your Homework •
Enjoy Investing

Sources of Information   **229**
Mutual-Funds Newsletters • Mutual-Funds
Statistical Services • Mutual-Funds Books
• Employee Benefits

Index   **235**

FIGURES

Figure 1.1   26 Years of Stock Market History   6

Figure 1.2   Quarterly Variability of High- and Low-Risk Funds 1986–1989   11

Figure 1.3   Nonmarket Risk Reduction   13

Figure 1.4   All-Weather Portfolio   16

Figure 1.5   Best Mix   19

Figure 2.1   Investment Pyramid   35

Figure 3.1   U.S. Stocks versus Foreign Stocks   50

Figure 3.2   U.S. Bond Market versus International Bond Market   55

Figure 4.1   The Industrial Life Cycle   73

Figure 5.1   Comparison of $10,000 Investment in Two Mutual Funds Each Growing Ten Percent Per Year, Compounded Annually   112

Figure 5.2   How to Read Newspaper Quotations   113

Figure 8.1   Dollar Cost Averaging versus Buy and Hold   167

Figure 9.1   Alternative Investment Strategies Over the Ten Years Ending 7/31/88   174

Figure 9.2   Formula Investing Strategies Over the Ten Years Ending 6/30/88   177

Figure 10.1 Distribution of Five-year Coin-Flip Returns   189

Figure 10.2 Distribution of Five-year Mutual-Funds Returns   190

TABLES

Table 1.1   Annual Returns of Assets   18
Table 2.1   Balance Sheet   24
Table 2.2   Income versus Expenses   26
Table 2.3   What $100 a Month Grows to   30
Table 2.4   Investment Profile   36
Table 3.1   Percentage Change in Bond Prices in
             Response to Changes in Interest Rates   41
Table 3.2   Correlations   42
Table 3.3   Diversification Mix Based on How Much
             Risk You Want to Take   43
Table 3.4   Real Rates of Return   53
Table 4.1   Common Stock versus Treasury Bill
             Returns   65
Table 4.2   Spotlight on Maximum Loss Periods   68
Table 4.3   Comparison of Future Growth Rates   77
Table 4.4   Estimated Earnings Growth   79
Table 4.5   Growth Stocks to Buy   82
Table 4.6   Good Blue-Chip Stocks   88
Table 4.7   Dividend-Paying Nationally Traded
             Companies   90
Table 4.8   Tried-and-True Companies   92
Table 4.9   Funds' Annual Growth Rate   95
Table 4.10   Bond Ratings   102
Table 5.1   Best Managed Stock Funds Annual Rate
             of Return %   126

Table 5.2   Best Managed Bond Funds Annual Rate
             of Return %   128
Table 7.1   Lipper—Mutual Fund Performance
             Analysis—Performance Summary   147
Table 7.2   Asset-Allocation Comparison   148
Table 7.3   Asset-Allocation Funds   150
Table 8.1   Dollar Cost Averaging with Vanguard
             Index 500   163
Table 9.1   Stock- and Bond-Fund Trades   173
Table 9.2   Rebalancing Cuts Risk, Increases
             Return   182
Table 10.1   S&P 500 versus T-Bills   191

PREFACE

Almost everyone is an astute investor when there is a bull market. People forget that stock market corrections exist. They buy hot mutual funds and stocks, watch their stocks rise in price, and spend their weekends counting their money.

Of course, all of that changes once the stock market plunges. It does that from time to time. We have experienced two severe setbacks over the past five years. In October of 1987 many investors saw the market value of their holdings drop 25 percent or more. Some sold, while others held on, figuring that the market would rebound eventually and they would recover their money.

Needless to say, stocks bounced back after the 1987 crash. Over the past five years that S&P 500 grew at an annual rate of nearly 14 percent.

The rebound, however, did not occur without another setback. In September of 1990 we had another steep correction. The dividend yield on the market fell to 4 percent from a high of 3 percent. Some mutual fund investors experienced a 20 to 30 percent drop in their aggressive equity funds that month. Fortunately, the market bounced back again.

Although most investors held on to their investment during the 1987 and 1990 corrections, most failed to add to their financial asset holdings—to diversify and thus cushion blows from another severe stock market decline that may occur in the future.

It's easy to cast stones now, but the most common mistake made by individual investors during the tail end of the great bull market was they ignored investment risk. They bought with the hope of making big money without diversifying or considering how much they were willing to lose. Individuals who invested heavily during 1986 and early 1987, hoping to amass a quick fortune, got singed. Those few investors who believed that they had found a money machine by writing naked options (a high-risk way to gamble on big profits without owning stock) got roasted. Thousands of these stories are about people who tripled their money. The greed fed on itself. As stock prices continued to rise, most investors were lured into investing more of their wealth into the stock market and into assets that were just too risky for the average person. When the roller coaster took its final breathtaking dip, a great many investors were unprepared for the shock: a 500-point decline on the Dow Jones Industrial Average on October 19, 1987.

Since the Crash, brokers have experienced difficulty pitching hot stocks and mutual funds. Investors remember getting burned a few years ago and now are extremely cautious. Stock brokers, like the Maytag repairman, became some of the loneliest people in town. In an effort to boost sagging commissions, brokers latched on to a new gimmick or sales pitch labeled "asset allocation." They are advising investors to split up investments among stocks, bonds and cash, thus protecting themselves in the event that stocks plunge.

Why didn't they advise investors to do that before? They were receiving too much in commissions selling hot investments. Even the mutual-funds industry is promoting asset allocation. Portfolios that once were called balance funds and included a stock, bond or cash split now are called asset-allocation funds.

Good investment advisors consider what investors want and then give them advice. Right now people want safety and long-term growth from their investments. They do not want to be caught with most of their investments in stocks only to find the market falling out of bed when the next recession rolls around. Brokers are advising investors to allocate among stocks, bonds and cash. To us, however, a "true" asset allocator is one who invests in a number of different assets to reduce risk and yet still earn acceptable investment returns.

Institutional money managers and financial researchers in the "halls of ivy" have been aware of the virtues of asset allocation for years. Simply put, asset allocation requires splitting up investments among several different types of asset classes, such as U.S. stocks and bonds, overseas stocks and bonds, precious metals and real estate. A portfolio is based on how much risk a person is willing to take or how much a person can lose in any given year without losing a good night's sleep. Asset allocation works because the returns among assets are uncorrelated, that is, while the returns from one asset class may be decreasing, the returns from others may be increasing. As a result, asset-allocated portfolios contain less price-performance variability or risk than those that concentrate in a single category of assets such as stocks.

Common stocks, over the long term, do provide investors with the best returns compared with bonds and T-bills. Stocks, however, also are the most risky. During several bear markets since the 1929 stock market crash, the stock market has dropped 50 percent or more. Knowing stock prices will rebound from a crash provides little consolation to many investors who help-lessly watched their hard-earned assets lose half their value. Some of these investors jumped out of the stock market at precisely the wrong time—they sold only to see stocks rebound.

Earning long-term rates of return requires a person to survive the volatile short term. The solution to this problem is to moderate gyrating stock market returns by investing in a portfolio of assets whose returns are relatively uncorrelated—to engage in asset allocation to receive the best returns with the least amount of risk.

This is what this book is about: the benefits of asset allocation. You will learn how to allocate your invest-ments to match your level of risk and still receive a decent return on your money. You will see how to split up the investment pie the way the money pros have done it for years to receive higher returns from lower-risk investments.

GERALD W. PERRITT
ALAN LAVINE

Acknowledgments

The authors would like to thank some of the people who helped make this book possible. Special thanks to Jennifer Brown and Suzanne Paola for reading and commenting on the manuscript. Alan Lavine thanks his editors for their support and encouragement through the years. Many thanks to Bill Castle, financial editor at the *Boston Herald,* Thomas Siedell, senior editor at *Your Money,* a Consumer Digest, Inc., publication, and John Wasik, senior editor, *Consumers' Digest.* Also a word of gratitude to Robert Belson for assisting in the research work that made this a super book.

PART
1

Why Diversify?

CHAPTER 1

What Is Asset Allocation?

DON'T BET THE RANCH ON A SINGLE HAND: DIVERSIFICATION REDUCES RISK

"**O**ctober. This is one of the peculiarly dangerous months to speculate in stocks. The others are July, January, September, April, November, May, March, June, December, August and February" (Mark Twain, in *Pudd'nhead Wilson*).

The more things change, the more they stay the same. October, for some reason, truly is a horrendous month for stocks. This ill-fated month kicked off the Great Depression with the Crash of 1929. Fifty-eight years later, the stock market bubble burst again while the leaves changed, and one trillion dollars were lost in one day on Wall Street in an October.

We got nailed in October of 1987. Almost two years later we took another licking. Aggressive stock fund investors lost almost 30 percent from August through September of 1990. The market subsequently rebounded. But who wants to invest a lump sum in a hot mutual fund that promptly loses one third of its value.

3

If we have learned anything from the stock market crash of October, 1987, it's that everyone must diversify. Besides federally insured bank accounts, there are no "safe" places to invest. You might think you are being cautious by investing in U.S. Treasury securities because Uncle Sam backs these bonds with "full faith and credit." Bond prices, however, move in opposition to interest rates, which means that if interest rates rise, bond prices drop and the market value of your holdings declines. The sensible answer? Divide investments into a wide range of assets and spread your risks against falling stock and bond prices. This way, for example, if stocks perform poorly, these losses can be offset by safer investments, such as bonds or money funds.

Though the crash was a bitter lesson, perhaps we can put that painful experience to good use. Now more than ever, investors want to play it safe with their hard-earned investment dollars. A 25-percent gain is intoxicating but futile if it evaporates before the investor can turn paper into actual profit, as happens more often than not. If you lose 25 percent, on the other hand, you have to make 33 percent to break even. And that could take years to accomplish.

According to a survey conducted by the Investment Company Institute, a Washington, D.C., mutual-funds trade organization, investors are more concerned about safety now than they have been in years—with good reason. They look for comfort instead of flashy returns. They feel, however, that they lack the knowledge to protect their money and still profit from investing.

BABY BOOMERS GOT BURNED

Some of us were introduced to investing when we opened a money-fund account back in the early 1980s. With little risk or effort, we earned double-digit returns. In 1981, the average money fund earned 16.8 percent.

That seemed easy enough, so why not dabble in stocks? In August of 1982, when interest rates dropped from double digits to below ten percent, we saw one of the greatest stock market rallies in recent investment history. Some small stock mutual funds gained 100 percent in 12 months. With minor deviations, the bull surged on until 1987. Hot tips multiplied like mushrooms on rainy summer nights. Everyone became a savvy investor.

Bernard Baruch, one of the all-time great financial thinkers, learned his lesson in the stock market crash of 1929. He warned others prior to the crash that "When beggars and shoeshine boys, barbers and beauticians can tell you how to get rich, it's time to remind yourself that there's no more dangerous illusion than the belief that one can get something for nothing."

By midsummer of 1987, stocks had grown at a prodigious rate of almost 30 percent a year. It looked like the blue skies over the Big Board would glow forever. The Dow Jones Industrial Average hit 2700 by August (see Figure 1.1) and the 30 largest industrial stocks that make up this index were up 41 percent year-to-date.

Nothing lasts forever, unfortunately, except death and taxes. On October 19, 1987, the stock market dropped 500 points, falling 40 percent from its high and closing out the year with a measly gain of only two percent. The stock market subsequently has rebounded, gaining back all that it lost during late 1987. This rebound affords small consolation to the many investors who, attracted by soaring returns, bought stocks at the end of August and lost 28 percent by the end of October! Those investors nearing retirement who had invested most of their money in equities saw a third of their future income evaporate before they sold, in a blind panic to avoid losing everything.

On the other hand, some savvy investors managed to escape the repercussions of the market plunge. Those who diversified, keeping just a third of their portfolios in stocks, bonds and cash, weathered the stock shock.

Figure 1.1   26 Years of Stock Market History

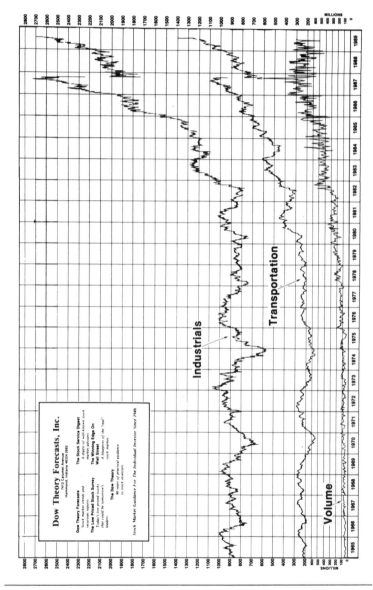

Source: Dow Theory Forecast, Inc.

From August 20, 1987, through October 29, 1987, for example, the Standard & Poor's 500 stock market index dropped 27 percent. A person who had 33 percent of his or her assets in growth stocks, bond and money-market mutual funds would have lost only nine percent during that period.

That hypothetical investor is a good example of why asset allocation or diversification is important. The aim of this strategy is to cut losses on the downside and still position enough funds in different markets to profit. The idea is to receive the best return with the least amount using the simplest investment strategy—buying and holding investments that are safe and that can potentially produce higher returns.

Diversification saved the day in 1990. If you put one third of your money in stocks, bonds and money funds you were up about 6 percent year-to-date ending in the third quarter of 1990. By contrast, the S&P 500 was down 11 percent. The average stock fund lost 13 percent after Iraq invaded Kuwait. Equity funds that invest worldwide lost about the same. However, money funds paid 7 percent interest and global bond funds appreciated 8 percent.

Our hypothetical investor who remained diversified during these troubled financial times is a good example of why asset allocation or diversification is important.

Pension-fund portfolio managers have been allocating assets for years to cut the risk of unexpected stock and bond market declines. These managers work their computers overtime to determine the lowest-risk investment mix, based on their outlook for the economy, interest rates, inflation and the financial markets.

You can use several of the prudent professional tactics to protect your investments and retirement savings. You will become rich a little more slowly, perhaps, than those who sink their assets into commodities straddles at propitious moments, but asset allocation is an attrac-

ADDISON PUBLIC LIBRARY
ADDISON, ILLINOIS

tive way to invest for several other important reasons, besides diversification:

- First, the practice encourages long-term investing. You must invest for a long enough period to take advantage of several business cycles. Diversification is not a perfect way to hedge, but over time it will work.
- Second, the guesswork of trying to time investment decisions based on changing financial conditions is eliminated. Your portfolio is positioned to protect you against all types of investment climates, such as high inflation, rising interest rates or the impact of a recession on stock prices.
- Third, it enables you to peg your tolerance for risk to a specifically mixed portfolio. You are able to change your investments throughout your life to anticipate changing needs. Younger people generally want to build their wealth by placing a larger proportion of their investments in equities. As these investors age and accumulate more wealth, they will look for less risk and for investment protection. When they retire, they will seek the maximum income obtainable from their portfolio without having to worry about defaults in the bond market or loss of purchasing power caused by rising inflation.

Before we look at how to allocate or diversify your investments, you must understand several important concepts.

YOU MUST CONSIDER THE RISKS

When you buy securities, you face two important risks.

Market risk is the risk that is common to all securities of the same class, such as stocks and bonds. Your stock's or bond's performance tracks the performance of the overall market. For example, stock prices rally because of good news about the economy. The S&P 500 gains five percent in one week. If you check the returns on your individual stocks or mutual funds, you will notice that these investments are up about five percent or a little more. If interest rates rise over a few weeks because of concerns about inflation, you will notice that suddenly your bond or fixed-income fund's price has declined.

Unless you hold different asset classes, you cannot diversify against market risk. According to financial research, about one-third of a stock's price movement is caused by the general movement of the market.

CORPORATE PROFITS IMPORTANT

Market risk is a result of expectations about future movements of corporate profits. If the financial news indicates that higher interest rates could drive us into a recession, stock prices may tumble. If the news suggests that corporate profits will increase because the federal government plans to lower interest rates in order to spur the economy, this is a positive development for corporate profits, and thus for stock prices.

INFLATION

When investors worry about inflation, prices of gold stocks and precious metals often rise as investors buy hard assets that will appreciate along with inflation. Conversely, bond prices will rise to compensate debt holders for their loss in purchasing power. Bond prices and interest rates, however, move in opposite directions, so if interest rates rise, bond prices will drop. In addition, the longer the term to maturity on a bond, the greater the price decline. If interest rates fall, bond prices rally.

PRICE VOLATILITY

You can obtain a professional measure of the market risk of your investment. *Beta value* is a statistical measure that tells you how a portfolio of securities will react to day-to-day moves in the overall markets. The S&P 500, which is an index that often is used to gauge the performance of the entire stock market, has a beta value of 1.0. If you own a portfolio of stocks or a mutual fund with a beta value of 1.2, your investment on an average will move 20 percent higher than the whole market during upward swings and 20 percent lower during downward swings. A portfolio with a beta of .50 would gain only half as much on the upside but lose only half as much on the downside.

You can receive a stock's or mutual fund's beta value from your stockbroker or mutual-fund service representative. Several directories also list beta values. The Value Line Investment Survey carries betas on thousands of stocks. CDA/Wiesenbergers' Mutual Fund Update lists betas for more than 1,000 funds.

Once you know a stock's or mutual fund's beta value, you possess a powerful tool for minimizing the risk of loss. You might decide to place half of your money in the Fidelity Capital Appreciation Fund, which sports a racy beta of 1.5, but as long as you divide the rest of your investment pie into bonds and money funds, the average beta value will drop to a very acceptable .75. You've provided yourself with a position in the equity market in case stocks take off and a protective cushion in case they don't.

A high beta will give you a wild ride. One with a low beta that balances investments between stocks, bonds, and cash does not fluctuate so much. Look how a high and low risk fund performed in every quarter before, during and after the stock market crash of 1987. In Figure 1.2, for example, you can see that if you invested in the 20th Century Growth Fund, you can win and lose a lot. Over the long term this fund has been an outstanding performer, but as a single investment, you can see

Figure 1.2   **Quarterly Variability of High- and Low-Risk
              Funds 1986–1989**

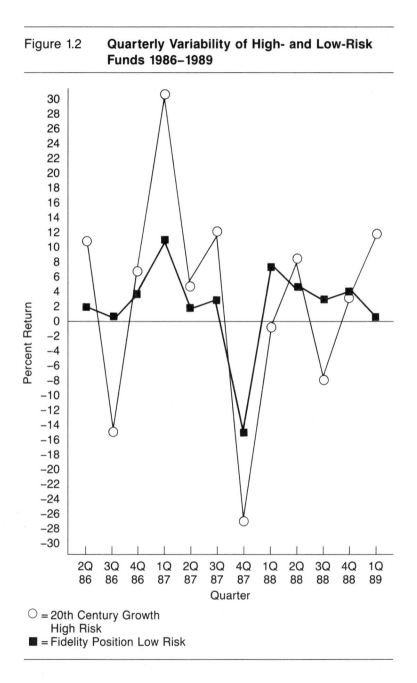

○ = 20th Century Growth
    High Risk
■ = Fidelity Position Low Risk

wide oscillations in the market value of the fund. In contrast, the Fidelity Balanced Fund offers less risk, for there is less quarterly volatility from 1986 through 1989.

Nonmarket risk is risk that is specific to a company or industry. Research shows that 60 percent of a common stock's return or risk is caused by positive or negative news about the company or its industry. For example, the Chief Economic Officer of a corporation unexpectedly dies or analysts forecast that housing-industry profits will drop ten percent next year because of high interest rates. The share prices in the company or industry suddenly will dive, and investors will lose money.

HOLD A LOT OF DIFFERENT INVESTMENTS

You can diversify against nonmarket risk by holding a number of different securities from different industries. In this way, you protect yourself against losses in a few securities because of unique events that can change a firm's profitability or performance. To accomplish this diversification within a specific class of assets, you must own 10 to 25 stocks from different industries. In this way, if one issue is hit hard because of bad news, the losses will be offset by the performance of the rest of the portfolio. If stocks are bought in round lots of 100 shares, you will need about $50,000 to $100,000 to diversify against nonmarket risk with individual securities.

Here is how diversification against nonmarket risk works. Assume that you own 100 shares of the following: Citicorp, which you bought at $22 per share; IBM, at $104; Phelps Dodge, at $53; and Commonwealth Energy, at $32.

You spent $21,100 assembling this portfolio, and your average share price is $52.75. Six months later, you rifle through the financial pages and see with a fair amount of pleasure that your stocks are trading at: CitiCorp, $25; IBM, $121; Phelps Dodge, $48; and Commonwealth Energy, $31.

Figure 1.3 **Nonmarket Risk Reduction**

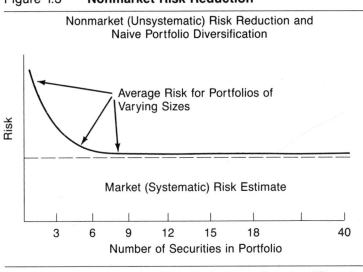

Nonmarket (Unsystematic) Risk Reduction and
Naive Portfolio Diversification

Source: J.L. Evans and S.H. Archer, "Diversification and the Reduction of Dispersion:
An Empirical Analysis", *Journal of Finance*, December 1968.

The market value of your Phelps Dodge and Commonwealth Energy holdings declined $500 and $100, respectively. The value of your Citicorp and IBM stocks, however, more than covered the loss, increasing $300 and $1,700, respectively.

Remember that if you have a large portfolio, 90 percent of its value will move with the market, which is a natural correlation that no investor can avoid. If a few stocks plummeted because of bad news, but the rest of your portfolio held its ground or increased in value, your losses would be cushioned.

The rule of thumb with diversification is that the greater the number of stocks contained in a portfolio, the lower the portfolio risk. The greater number of stocks you own, the less you will experience wide swings in returns. As you can see in Figure 1.3, the amount you can reduce risk by adding more stocks to your portfolio diminishes rather quickly. According to a study conducted by J. L. Evans and S. H. Archer in the *Journal of Finance,* you receive very little risk reduction when you add more than 15 stocks to a portfolio.

PROTECTION THROUGH DIVERSIFICATION

Another way to diversify against risk is to invest in different types of assets that perform differently during different economic conditions.

Correlation is a statistical measure that demonstrates the extent that the performance of different investments move in tandem. It measures a degree of association. Simply put, if two investments have a 100 percent correlation, for example, their prices always move very closely in the same direction. If two investments have a 50 percent correlation, then half the time they move together and half the time they move in opposite directions or don't move together. If there is a −1.0 correlation, the two assets move in opposite directions. T-bills, for instance, have a negative correlation of −.06 with stocks, which means there is virtually no relationship or not even an opposite relationship to the stock market.

Correlation of investment returns is important to reducing risk. The lower the correlation of returns among assets, the greater the benefit of diversification. Consider, for example, two assets whose returns move in opposite directions. They both might be risky investments, but when placed in the same portfolio, the losses incurred by one asset are offset by gains in the other. The result: The total price volatility is less than either asset.

HEDGING YOUR BETS

If you are going to put together a portfolio that includes stocks and you want to diversify, then you must hedge by investing in assets that do not move in tandem with stocks. For example, bonds, precious metals and T-bills all boast low correlations with stocks. Even foreign stock prices only move in tandem with U.S. stocks about 40 percent of the time, but tend to provide similar returns. By dividing up the investment pie among U.S. and foreign stocks, bonds, T-bills or money funds and precious metals, you can build an all-weather portfolio.

If you study the investment returns of a number of assets over time, you can see how correlation works to protect your hard-earned dollars; diversification works via correlation. In 1969, for example, stocks lost 8.5 percent, but foreign stocks and gold registered positive returns of 6.4 percent and 5.6 percent. Investors lost some money in bonds, but in 1974, when stocks dropped 26.5 percent, bonds registered 4.4 percent gains. In the same year, foreign stocks tumbled 24 percent, but losses were offset in real estate and gold.

THE HIGH PRICE OF TOGETHERNESS

This correlation, or "togetherness measure," is a critical concept to diversification. In a financial portfolio, compatibility depends on avoiding togetherness. By mixing investments that have low correlations with one another, you are protecting your portfolio against major losses.

For instance, you want to put together an all-weather, diversified portfolio. You look at the correlations among different assets and divide your money among the assets that have the lowest correlations to each other—and thus the ability to counteract each other. In chapter 3, we will cover this in more detail. Some stock market exposure is desirable because you want growth, but you also want protection. You may come up with a portfolio that consists of perhaps 15 percent blue-chip stocks, 15 percent over-the-counter growth stocks, 15 percent overseas stocks, 15 percent domestic bonds, 20 percent international bonds, 5 percent gold and 15 percent money funds.

Figure 1.4   **All-Weather Portfolio**

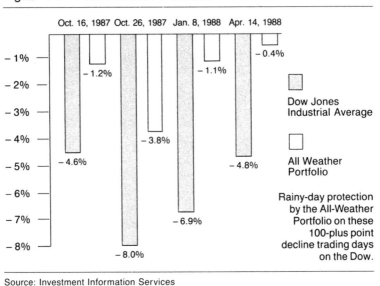

Source: Investment Information Services

With this portfolio you would have weathered the shock of October, 1987, and smiled—maybe a little grimly—while others wept. Figure 1.4 shows a day-by-day performance analysis. On October 16, 1987, the Dow lost 4.6 percent, but your all-weather portfolio dropped just 1.2 percent. On October 26, 1987, the Dow lost 8.0 percent, while the all-weather portfolio declined just 3.8 percent. On January 8, 1988, the Dow fell 6.9 percent, although the all-weather portfolio lost just 1.1 percent. These gaps provide telling examples of what correlation and diversification are all about.

HIGH RETURN WITH LOWER RISK

Risk Versus Return.   Some securities are riskier than others, which means that their prices tend to swing widely in relation to the rest of the market. Often, the bigger the risk, the bigger the potential return because of that price volatility. You could realize a 25 percent return quickly with a hot stock or mutual fund, but you could lose just as much just as quickly. The riskiness of a security is much like its margin of error. In statistics, this margin of error also is known as a standard deviation; we will use the term *margin of error*. Historically, stocks have registered an average annual return of ten percent since 1926. This does not mean, of course, that stock market investors earn a guaranteed ten percent return every year. Stock prices can be up 15 percent in one year, down 12 percent in another, up five percent the next and down two percent in the following year. If you average up the total gains and divide by the number of years recorded, however, you will show a consistent ten percent.

Because prices always fluctuate, you must figure out your own margin of error—the average price swing over time of your investments. Stocks have a margin of error of 21 percent. They average ten percent, but the range in any given period can be 31 percent or –11 percent, based on statistical calculations. Thirty-one and –11 divided by two equals ten percent.

The annual return on Government Bonds is 4.9 percent with a margin of error of 8.6 percent. In any given year, you can expect to earn between 13.5 percent and –4.3 percent. T-bills, beloved of the risk-averse, average a 3.7 percent return with a margin of error of 3.3 percent. (See Table 1.1.)

You can combine lower-risk investments with higher ones to maximize the advantages of both. In later chapters, you will find tables that will help you choose the best mix of high- and low-risk investments.

Graphically, however, you can see how this mixing of investments works to give you the return you want with the lowest amount of risk. By plotting the average return of the vertical axis and the margin of error or

---

Table 1.1   Annual Returns of Assets

Asset Class	Time	Geo. Mean %	Standard Deviation %
S&P 500	1/26–12/92	10.3	20.6
Small Stocks	1/26–12/92	12.0	39.6
Foreign Stocks	1/60–12/92	12.8	20.0
Government Bonds	1/26–12/92	4.9	8.6
Corporate Bonds	1/26–12/92	5.5	8.5
U.S. T-bills	1/26–12/92	3.7	3.3
Foreign Bonds	1/60–12/92	8.7	10.1
Inflation	1/26–12/92	3.1	4.7

Sources: Ibbotson Associates, Chicago; Institutional Property Consultants, San Diego.

---

risk measure on the horizontal axis, as in Figure 1.5, we create a picture of risk versus return.

If you look at the points on the graph, you will see where they fall in terms of return and risk. Point A demonstrates that small stocks afford the highest return and also the highest risk. The S&P 500 falls on point B, followed by foreign stocks on point C, foreign bonds on point D, T-bills on point E and bonds on point F.

What investment would you pick? You might like the idea of earning 17 percent but know realistically that you cannot tolerate the big price fluctuations. If you expect you might need cash, you would stand a good chance of selling at a loss. You do not want to put all your money in T-bills, however, and average the comparative pittance of 3.5 percent a year.

Suppose, however, you mixed together small stocks, large stocks, foreign bonds and T-bills because they have low correlations with each other. You would receive a higher return, with less risk, than if you invested 100 percent in highly volatile over-the-counter small growth stocks! By simply quartering your portfolio, you'd create

Figure 1.5   **Best Mix**

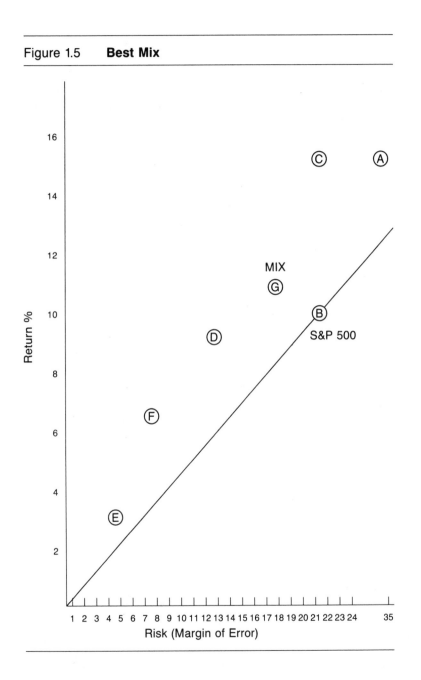

an investment at point G. You could expect an average return (based on historical data) of 8.6 percent with a margin of error of 17. Your investment would earn more than T-bills or government bonds, while staying less risky than U.S. or foreign stocks. Your annual downside risk would be ten percent, with a 24 percent upside ceiling—plenty of room for growth, but with reasonable risk.

INVESTING TO WIN, PLACE AND SHOW

Asset allocation is like horse racing. Bet $50 on Baystate Kate at 20 to 1 and you could make $1,000, if she wins. Chances are that the long shot will limp around the entire six furlongs and come in last. If you bet the favorite to win, place and show, however, you've hedged your bet. Sound boring? Kentucky Derby winner Sunday Silence paid $3 for coming in third place; you would have won $1 on a $2 bet—not so exciting as winning at 20-to-1 odds, maybe, but still a 50 percent rate of return in a single afternoon.

Only the odds makers get rich at the racetrack. Investors can, however, profit from bet-hedging strategies. All of these statistics serve to explain one simple fact: Asset allocation works. It's academic. All you must do is divide up your portfolio to win, place and show.

CHAPTER 2

What Is Your Level of Risk?

You must have a financial game plan in place before you begin diversifying your investments. Once you've figured out a budget and determined how much you must save, you should assess how much risk you can handle to achieve your financial goals.

ZEROING IN ON YOUR FINANCIAL NEEDS AND GOALS

The United States Treasury makes money the old-fashioned way. They print it. For the average citizen who does not have access to the federal government's printing press, however, the only way to build wealth is to start a savings plan. Such a step means cutting the fat out of your budget and taking a hard look at your financial goals.

Financial pressures, needless to say, are worrisome. As Joe Louis, the world champion boxer, once said, "I don't like money, but it quiets my nerves." Most of us need to run our financial affairs more efficiently for the sake of more than our nerves.

After inflation and taxes, the nine percent average annual return on your Flying Wallendas High Yield Bond Fund translates into a mere two percent, even during these disinflationary years. And unless you've inherited a few hundred thousand dollars, it may take some footwork to meet your financial goals. By the time a young child is ready for college in 10 to 15 years, four years of higher education will cost about $60,000. Suppose you want to receive $35,000 in annual income, in addition to your social security, by the time you retire. You'll have to amass a retirement fund of more than $335,000, which would take 25 years, assuming your investment earns 8.25 percent and you're able to put $4,000 a year into a retirement savings plan.

PAY YOURSELF FIRST

This $300,000 is a hefty IOU to face over the next couple of decades. The biggest step toward reaching your goal is to realign your priorities now, by paying yourself first. The late Andre Meyer, an investment banker and counsel to world leaders, amassed a $400 million personal fortune. He didn't invest in high-flying growth stocks or junk bonds. All he did was follow the simple philosophy of "accumulate and preserve." Meyer took his racy million-dollar fees and socked them away in conservative bank accounts, Treasury securities, bonds and blue-chip stocks.

ACCUMULATE MONEY

While you probably don't have a million dollars to salt away every year, you still can follow Meyer's advice. For instance, you paid yourself an extra $100 a month because you cut wasteful spending and you invested the money at eight percent a year, over 20 years you could boast an extra $60,000 in "found" money. If your investment pool averaged ten percent a year, your stash would be worth $76,569. At an annual rate of 12 percent, which is highly possible when you consider that, over the past 60 years, stocks have grown at that annual rate, you'd find yourself with $100,000—all from bypassing two or three dinners out a month!

FINDING MONEY TO INVEST

Make a list of your short-term, intermediate and long-term goals, along with the date and estimated cost of meeting those objectives. Short-term goals might include saving three to six months' income as an emergency fund or for that down payment on a car. Intermediate goals might include items such as a house down payment or educational expenses. Over the long term, you probably would be saving for retirement.

HOW MUCH ARE YOU WORTH?

Next you must determine how much you are worth. Create a balance sheet listing your assets and liabilities. Assets are what you own; liabilities are what you owe. The balance sheet would look like Table 2.1.

CUT THE FAT OUT OF THE FAMILY BUDGET

After you've determined what you're worth, look at your budget or income less expenses. According to most financial planners, you must save from 5 to 15 percent of your gross income to meet future financial needs. Start by writing down, item by item, all the money you spend in a week. You'll be surprised at how much it adds up to—that extra cup of coffee at the diner around the corner, magazines, the sawbuck you bet on the Chicago Cubs to beat

---

Table 2.1   Balance Sheet

Assets

Financial assets:
Cash and checking accounts   _____
Savings accounts   _____
Certificates of deposit   _____
Stocks and bonds   _____
Life insurance cash value   _____
Mutual funds   _____
Collections   _____
Real estate   _____
Loans owed to you   _____
Other   _____
Total Financial Assets   _____

Nonliquid assets:
Home   _____
Automobile   _____
Household furnishings   _____
Equity in business   _____
Other   _____
Total Fixed Assets   _____

Future assets
Company pension   _____
IRA   _____
Keogh   _____
Other   _____
Total Future Assets   _____
Grand Total Assets   _____

Liabilities
Home mortgage   _____
Other real estate   _____
Installment credit:

24

Automobile	_____
Furniture	_____
Home improvement	_____
Education	_____
Clothing	_____
Other debts	_____
Total Liabilities	_____
Net Worth (assets less liabilities)	_____

the Dodgers. Next, leaf through your checkbook and make an itemized list of income and expenses for the year, then divide it by 12 for a monthly figure. Once you've determined exactly where you're spending, figure out where you can cut. Your budget will look like Table 2.2.

RECLAIM WASTEFUL SPENDING

Once you've completed the balance sheet and budget, look for places where extra money for investment may be found. Perhaps your balance sheet shows that your debts are growing faster than your assets. In that case, you'll have to start building your wealth. If you're in the red every month, or for several months, ask yourself why. Perhaps you had a financial emergency such as a leaky roof. Or maybe you've been making unnecessary purchases because everyone you know has a European car or a does-everything-but-talk home-entertainment system. Either way, the budget should show you where you can cut nonessential spending to free up money to invest. Once you've decided how much you must save every month, stick to your new budget and keep close tabs on spending.

Table 2.2   Income Versus Expenses

Income

Take-home pay   _____

Other income   _____

Fixed monthly expenses

Savings and investing   _____

House or rent   _____

Automobile and transportation   _____

Other debt payments   _____

Food   _____

Utilities   _____

Child care   _____

Other   _____

Subtotal   _____

Variable monthly expenses

Tax payment   _____

Insurance payment   _____

House repairs   _____

Automobile repairs   _____

Medical   _____

Other   _____

Subtotal   _____

Total Monthly Expenses   _____

Extra (income less expenses)   _____

COMPARE LAST YEAR'S EXPENSES TO THIS YEAR'S

One way to get a quick bead on needless spending is to compare what you've spent with a specific budget plan—the actual versus the hypothetical. Look at the following annual percentages of how much, after taxes, you should be spending on line items in your budget. These percentages aren't immutable, of course. Adjust them to meet local conditions. Pull out last year's tax return and multiply your after-tax income by each of these percentages. Divide by 12 for a hypothetical monthly budget, then compare these figures to actual monthly expenses and subtract the difference. Areas where you've gone over budget are areas where you should trim the fat.

You should spend about:

- 25 to 30 percent of your income on housing, including interest, principle and taxes;
- 13 percent on food;
- six percent on life insurance;
- six percent on transportation;
- not more than 20 percent in credit cards and installment debt;
- five percent on entertainment;
- six percent on clothing;
- 5 to 20 percent paid to yourself for savings; and
- medical expenses would vary with your age and health.

WHERE TO CUT SPENDING

After comparing what you spend with a budget, you'll find that you can save a lot of money by cutting impulse buying at the grocery store and the department store. You also can free up extra cash to invest by trimming entertainment expenses, using the public library rather than paying $7 for a paperback, and possibly commuting to work instead of taking your car into town. In addition, you often can save money by refinancing your mortgage when interest rates decline. If you're paying too much in credit-card charges, pay off the debt—it's a painful but financially laudable move. If you can't, then consolidate your debts by getting a secured loan at the bank. Banks charge about two percent more interest than the collateral would earn in a CD, which is far lower than the usurious annual rate on most credit cards. A bank loan can cut interest-rate payments by as much as five percent a year over credit-card rates.

By taking these steps, you might find an extra $200 a month or more to invest. Regardless of what you can salvage from the wrack of necessity, the important move is to make up a budget and stick to it. If you feel you're in serious financial straits, too serious to control yourself, consider hiring a financial planner. You can write the International Association For Financial Planning (2 Concourse Parkway, Atlanta, GA 30328) for a free list of planners in your area.

MANAGING YOUR CASH AS A CORPORATE TREASURER WOULD

In addition to budgeting, there are other simple ways to free up investable cash. Corporate treasurers use efficient cash-management tactics to make their money work for them. Individuals can use some of the same principles when they invest.

Here are a few tips on how to manage your cash like a pro. By following these guidelines, you may be able to free up as much as $250 a year. That nifty sum eventually could pay for your son's or daughter's first year at graduate school. Over 20 years, earning just the pedestrian passbook savings rate of 5.5 percent, that $250 would grow to an extra $8,717—not a bad little bonus for your retirement. To start shaving these extra trifles from your budget, start a Now account at your local bank if you don't already have one and follow this plan:

- Deposit all your checks as soon as you receive them and make your deposits through a teller, not through an automated teller machine (ATM). At some banks, ATM deposits take an extra day to clear through the system.
- If you invest in CDs, check the bank's rollover policy. Some banks will pay lower rates for a short time, until you instruct them to reinvest the maturing funds.
- Make use of your employer's direct-payroll-deposit program. The money is electronically credited to your NOW account and earns interest immediately.
- Invest in an out-of-state money-market fund with check-writing privileges. If you pay your major local bills with a money fund, you could earn an extra few days' interest on your funds while your money-fund checks clear.
- Avoid bank charges. Be sure to keep at least the minimum required balance in your checking account or you may pay a monthly service fee of $8 to $10. If you have a bank money-market account, the bank might lower your interest rate if you slip below the required minimum.
- Charge smart. As long as you have no outstanding balance on your Visa or MasterCard, for example, you have about a 25-day grace period each month before the bill is due. Watch your billing cycle. Charge things toward the end of the cycle and you'll have a month to pay. That's 30 days' interest income you could earn before you pay your bills.
- Invest in no-load mutual funds, that is, funds with no up-front sales charges or hidden fees. Why pay an 8.5 to 4 percent up-front sales charge for the privilege of giving an investment company your

assets? Make all of your money work for you—not for your stockbroker.

- Year-end tax strategies also can save you money. Most Certified Public Accountants (CPAs) suggest you cut your year-end tax bill by deferring 1993 income to 1994 and accelerating deductions this year. Most state and local taxes require withholding and estimated payments. You should pay the full amount of the tax you owe before year-end, even though some of the tax may not be due until January or April of the following year.

Prepay your real-estate tax. If you have received a real-estate tax bill covering a 12-month period ending in 1994, you could pay it in full now and deduct it on your 1993 tax return. And don't forget to ask your employer to pay you your year-end bonus in January of the following year.

HOW MUCH WILL YOUR MONEY BE WORTH?

Once you've decided to set your financial game plan into action, you must determine how much your savings will grow. If you need money for a child's college education, that vacation home or an extra retirement-savings kitty, how much will you accumulate if you put $100 into an

Table 2.3 What $100 a Month Grows to

Percentage Return

Years	5	8	10	12	15
5	$ 6,829	7,397	7,808	8,247	8,968
10	15,592	18,417	20,655	23,334	27,866
15	26,840	34,835	41,792	50,458	67,686
20	41,275	59,295	76,570	99,915	151,595
25	59,799	95,737	133,789	189,764	328,407
30	83,573	150,030	227,933	352,991	700,982

account that earns 5 through 15 percent. If, for example, you will need an additional $40,000 to pay for your child's college education, check the compound interest table and you will see that if you put $100 a month in an investment that earned ten percent annually compounded monthly, you would have saved almost $42,000 for college.

THE INVESTMENT RISKS

To invest in the financial markets, you must understand investment risks, your own financial goals and your comfort level before you can build an all-weather portfolio. For instance, you face the following risks:

- Market timing. You could find yourself investing in bonds or stocks at a market peak, only to find the markets declining.
- Lost opportunity. Many investors like the safety of federally insured CDs, but buying CDs involves risk, too. You could find yourself locked into one as interest rates are rising.
- Credit risk. You could be attracted to the high yields offered by junk bonds with low credit ratings. During a recession, however, issuers with lower credit-rated companies may have a hard time paying back principal and interest to lenders.
- Interest-rate risk. Bond prices and interest rates move in opposite directions. If interest rates rise, bond prices decline. The longer the maturity on the bond, the greater the price drop. If, for example, interest rates rose one percent, your 20-year 9-percent bond would lose about ten percent of its market value. A short-term note with a maturity of ten years would lose about half that much.
- Diversification risk. If you don't plan your investments carefully, you could find yourself holding a

limited number or type of stocks or bonds unhedged. You might make big profits, but you'd have nothing to balance out potential losses.

THE INSOMNIA FACTOR

No one eliminates risk. The best way to protect your hard-earned assets is to diversify with stocks, bonds, money funds and precious metals. Before you decide how to diversify, ask yourself how much you would be willing to lose in a given year. Are you comfortable accepting a two- or four-percent loss? Could you handle losing six or eight percent in 1990? Maybe you could even accept a ten percent loss for the chance of earning 20 percent.

HOW MUCH ARE YOU WILLING TO LOSE?

Try answering the questions developed by Michael Lipper, president of Lipper Analytical Services in New York. Lipper's questionnaire is one of the best, because it clearly focuses on the risk-return relationship.

Take the risk test. If you score 5, you have a low tolerance for risk. A score of 10 means you're a moderate investor, while a score of 25 designates you as a risk taker. Circle your answers and add up the numbers.

- My investment is for the long term. The end result is more important than how I went about achieving it. (1) Totally disagree; (2) can accept variability, but not losses of capital; (3) can accept reasonable amounts of price fluctuation in total return; (4) can accept an occasional year of negative performance in the interest of building capital; (5) agree.
- Rank the importance of current income. (1) Essential and must be known; (2) essential but willing to accept uncertainty about the amount; (3) important,

but there are other factors to consider; (4) modest current income is desirable; (5) irrelevant.
- Rank the amount of decline you can accept in a single quarter. (1) None; (2) a little, but not for the entire year; (3) consistency of results is more important than outperformance; (4) a few quarters of decline is a small price to pay to be invested when the stock market takes off; (5) unimportant.
- Rank the importance of beating inflation. (1) Preservation of capital and income are more important; (2,3,4) willing to invest to beat inflation, but other investment needs come first; (5) essential to ensure that you get a real return on your investment.
- Rank the importance of beating the stock market over the economic cycle. (1) Irrelevant; (2,3,4) prefer consistency over superior results; (5) critical.

WHAT INVESTMENTS ARE RIGHT FOR YOU?

Once you've zeroed in on how much risk you're willing to take, you can start investigating what investments are right for you. You don't want to sink your funds in a go-go over-the-counter growth stock if you're averse to risk. Conversely, if you need growth for the long term, you don't want to invest in bonds for interest income. You must match the riskiness of investments with your objectives.

HOW RISKY IS RISKY?

The greater the potential payoff, the greater the risk. Investors are compensated for sticking their necks out. But how far?

Over the long term, a risky asset may produce a great yield record, but when times get tough, investors must sell because they need money, which drives down prices.

If you cannot hold on for the rebound, you are vulnerable. If you're not wiped out over the recessionary short term by the 16 percent high-yielding junk bond, however, you will collect a lot of interest income.

You must rank investments in terms of risk. Avoid the most risky investments, such as futures. You want to find the best mix of investments with the highest return and the least amount of risk.

HOW INVESTMENTS STACK UP

The investment pyramid in Figure 2.1 illustrates the most- and least-risky assets. Riskier investments, with the greatest price volatility, expose you to the greatest losses. Study this illustration before you start your diversified-investment plan.

At the top of the pyramid are the "boom or bust" investments. These might earn you 100 percent on your investment, or they might evaporate in front of your eyes. At the next level are investments in which you can expect to earn an average of 15 to 25 percent in any given year or lose as much as 20 percent. In the upper bottom half of the pyramid are mutual-funds investments. These funds hold a large number of issues and generally are considered safer than individual securities. Precious metals and over-the-counter-stock mutual funds, however, can be quite volatile performers. Mutual funds that invest in high-dividend blue-chip stocks are less risky, and balanced funds that keep half their assets in stocks and bonds are very conservative vehicles. At the bottom of the pyramid are the most-secure choices, such as government securities, which are guaranteed against default. Buyers do, of course, face interest-rate risk, as is the case with other low-risk investments, including short-term T-bills, federally insured bank CDs and money funds.

Figure 2.1   **Investment Pyramid**

Upper

- Commodity futures
- Strategic metals
- Options
- Lower credit-rated or "junk" bonds
- Gold and precious metals
- Sector mutual funds

Upper Middle

- Real-estate and equipment-leasing limited partnerships
- Speculative small-company growth stocks
- Blue-chip stocks
- Convertible bonds
- Investment-grade corporate bonds

Middle

- Precious-metals mutual funds
- Overseas stock and bond mutual funds
- Aggressive-stock mutual funds
- Growth-stock mutual funds
- Growth and income mutual funds
- Balanced mutual funds
- Corporate bond funds

Upper Lower

- U.S. federal-agency bond funds
- U.S. Treasury security bond funds
- Money-market mutual funds

Lower

- T-bills
- U.S. government-securities money fund
- Federally insured bank accounts and certificates of deposit.

CREATING AN INVESTMENT MIX: GETTING THE BEST RETURN WITH THE LEAST AMOUNT OF RISK

Now that you've got a feel for your investable money and your tolerance for risk, the next step is putting the pieces together.

First, you must look at an investment profile. This is the part of the pyramid that should be used to allocate assets. These investments offer a combination of safety, liquidity (the ability to gain immediate access to your cash), income and growth. Table 2.4 illustrates what investments best fit your needs.

Table 2.4 Investment Profile

Your Needs	Risk Level	Types of Investments
Safety, liquidity and yield	Very low	T-bills, bank CDs, money funds, bank accounts
Safety and yield	Low	Treasury notes, short-term bonds, government-agency securities, fixed-income mutual funds
Income	Low to moderate	Blue-chip high-dividend-yielding stocks or mutual funds, utility stocks, preferred stock
Growth	Higher	Gold, individual aggressive-growth stocks and mutual funds, high-yield bonds and funds, foreign securities

It seems that every financial advisor and his or her grandparent make asset-allocation recommendations these days. The preponderance of financial advice does not make finding your own special investment mix any easier. Different sources of investment wisdom may provide totally different answers to the question of how to meet your goals.

Who is right, if anyone? Can any one investment formula apply to everyone? Why would a widow living on a retirement stipend put half her money in stocks with an average annual price swing of plus or minus 21 percent? Why would a young professional making $50,000 a year want half of his or her income tied up in a conservative bond position? That professional probably wants long-term growth with a bit of diversification. A 30-year-old might well embrace stock-market risk because over the long term stocks have been rewarding investments.

YOUR COMFORT LEVEL

Any time you split up your investment among stocks, bonds and cash, however, you've made a good move, for any diversification is better than none. The best investment mix for you will be based partially on your own comfort level. If you cannot sleep at night because you are worrying about your $15,000 worth of undervalued up-and-coming growth stocks, the investment is not worth it, even if your balance sheet shows that it's the right thing to do.

CHAPTER 3

How to Split Up Your Investment Pie

One thing that you cannot do with your portfolio is divide it up and forget about it. Your risk level may change. You also may want to make a practice of rebalancing your portfolio annually to ensure that it stays in line with your investment philosophy. That way, you'll be sure you never have too much money at risk. If your stocks have risen 25 percent in value, for instance, and now represent half of your portfolio, you may want to shift some of the profits into bonds and money funds.

To find the right mix, you must consider the correlations among assets. These figures will show how often stocks, bonds, precious metals, and money funds move in the same or opposite directions. Following are the steps for getting a good estimate on your investment mix.

First, expand on the concept of the balanced fund because the stock-and-bond split provides a low-risk investment. You can re-create that type of split with different investments and receive an even better return with about the same risk as with a balanced fund.

Second, even growth-oriented investors consider investing in high-quality bonds or bond funds for several reasons. The annual income on bonds is fixed and therefore is predictable. In addition, because the bond principal is eventually returned to investors, bonds provide a means for capital preservation. When a bond matures, your initial investment is returned to you. You must recognize, however, that the $10,000 you invested ten years ago in a bond that matures today will not buy as many groceries as it did a decade ago. You get back some of your money, but also face purchasing-power risk.

A more compelling reason to invest in bonds today is that since the mid-1970s, widely fluctuating interest rates have made bonds ideal trading vehicles. Depending on your time horizon, you buy them when interest rates are high and sell them when rates decline. As can be seen in Table 3.1, a one percent or 200 basis point drop (100 basis points equals 1 percent) in interest rates would result in an 11 percent gain in the value of a 30 year Treasury bond. That's a little more than the average annual return on the stock market over the past six decades. By keeping a position in bond funds, you can use some of the increase volatility to boost your returns, but still retain downside protection in the form of interest income. The stream of cash flow from interest income enables you to set up an allocated portfolio with good risk-return characteristics.

You must consider this caveat in bond-market investing: It is difficult to time the markets, even for the money pros. Interest-rate timing is much harder than it appears on the surface, which is why you must look for professional management from advisors or bond funds before you take a position in this market. As Table 3.1 reveals, the percent change in a bond's value can be drastic depending on the maturity. Before you invest in a bond or bond fund, you must determine its responsiveness to changes in interest rates and thereby get an idea of the level of interest-rate risk you are assuming when you invest.

Table 3.1 Percentage Change in Bond Prices in Response to Changes in Interest Rates

Rate Change	Maturity (Years)				
(Basis points)	5	10	15	20	25
+200	−7.8	−12.9	−16.1	−18.3	−19.6
+100	−4.0	−6.7	−8.6	−9.9	−10.7
−100	+4.2	+7.3	+9.7	+11.5	+12.8
−200	+8.7	+15.4	+20.7	+24.0	+28.2

You also must make money funds an integral part of an allocated portfolio. Because you live in a world of volatile interest rates, money funds can serve as anchors in the portfolio for these funds maintain a net asset value or price per share of $1. Money-fund portfolio managers lengthen and shorten the maturity of their portfolios to increase their returns. When interest rates are rising, managers shorten the maturity of their investments so they can roll over maturing dollars into higher-rate products. When interest rates are declining, managers lengthen maturities to lock in higher yields. In addition, no risk of a price decline exists with money funds. With these funds in your portfolio, you will earn higher returns without experiencing the losses in bond funds when interest rates go up.

COMBINING ASSETS

Third, if you want some growth from the stock market along with safety, look down column 1 of Table 3.2 until you find the acceptable investments with the lowest correlations. You mix stocks, bonds, overseas securities, and money funds to realize the best return for each unit of risk or volatility.

Look down the aggressive-growth column until you find the lowest stock correlations. The first entry you will find is growth or growth and income funds with .978 and .931 relationships. Take the growth and income fund because it is slightly lower. The next items to follow are international stock funds at .743, precious metals funds at .187 and money funds at –.021—a ringer!

You want to combine assets that have the lowest correlations. Money funds don't earn much today. You will be lucky to earn 3 percent on your money for the entire year. That's not much. What's important is that money funds have a low correlation to stock fund performance. That can help when the stock market tumbles. A money fund position acts as an anchor and cushions the blow of a stock market correction.

Table 3.2 Correlations

	Agrw	Corpbd	Grth	G&inc	Inter	Metal	Mony
Agrw	1.00	.40	.99	.95	.80	.42	–.07
Corpbd	.40	1.00	.43	.51	.39	.07	.04
Grw	.99	.43	1.00	.98	.82	.42	–.09
Gr&i	.95	.51	.98	1.00	.81	.39	–.08
Inter	.80	.39	.82	.81	1.00	.51	–.13
Metal	.42	.07	.42	.39	.51	1.00	–.08
Mony	–.07	.04	–.09	–.08	–.13	–.08	1.00

Source: CDA

Now, you must come up with a good percentage mix—another leaner. See Table 3.3.

Table 3.3 Diversification Mix Based on How Much Risk You Want to Take

Type of investor	Grwstk	Grw&I	Bonds	Gold	Interstk	Money fund
Very low risk	0.5	4.5	10.5	1.0	9.0	73.5
Medium low	10.0	3.0	7.5	3.5	15.0	63.0
Moderate	11.0	9.0	5.0	6.0	23.0	46.0
Medium	22.5	10.5	3.0	10.0	34.0	20.0
High	29.5	9.5	1.0	11.0	43.0	6.0

Source: CDA

RISK AVERSE

Maybe you feel that you are somewhat risk averse, but you still want good long-term growth (doesn't everyone?). Place .5 percent of your assets in aggressive-growth funds, 4.5 percent in growth and income funds, 10.5 percent in bonds, 1 percent in gold, 9 percent in international stocks, and 73.5 percent in money funds.

If you were looking for moderate growth, you would divide up your funds with about 11 percent in aggressive-stock funds, 9 percent in growth and income funds, 5 percent in bond funds, 23 percent in international stock funds, 6 percent in metals funds and 46 percent in money funds. A higher-risk investor who wants a bigger position in stocks would place 29.5 percent in aggressive-stock funds, 9.5 percent in growth and income funds, 1 percent in bonds, 43 percent in international funds, 11 percent in metals funds and 6 percent in money funds.

Keep in mind that these tables are not written in stone. The percentage breakdowns are just guidelines. The most important thing is to split up the investment pie. If you divide up your investments in equal parts among the seven types of funds you will do well. You could expect to earn 86 percent of the return on the S&P 500 with about 40 percent less risk. You will not earn as much as the stock market when it goes up. Buy contrast, you will lose less when the market plunges.

YOUR FINANCIAL PASSAGES

One more step must be taken. The low-, moderate-, and higher-risk mixes are not enough. You also must analyze your own financial condition and the present stage of maturity of your financial life. Younger people usually want to see their wealth grow. Once these investors have matured and have accumulated a substantial amount of their net worth, they tend to concentrate on keeping it. Those nearing retirement still look for growth, but more safety, too. Retired people need safety, liquidity, and yield. Senior citizens on fixed incomes must be able to reach their cash in the event of a medical emergency; they also need the most interest income they can squeeze out of their bankers and stockbrokers.

HOW YOU SPLIT IT UP

Here is a suggested breakdown for you to consider. If the mixes seem too risky or too conservative, make your adjustments. You know how much risk you can tolerate and still get a good night's sleep.

The younger you are, the more risk you should be willing to take. Over the short run, you may experience greater declines in the market value of your portfolio, but time is the key: Time is one of the most valuable of investment commodities, and you have time on your side. The longer you hold on, the more you can make risk work for you when you are even partially invested in stocks. Conversely, once you have built up your wealth, you should protect it and provide for your retirement.

The following examples will show you how to split up the investment formula based on your age and financial status.

Example I. Young, single, 20 to 30 years old, more risk-oriented and interested in building capital over the long term. As long as you can ride out some bear markets by investing when prices go down, your investment should average about 15 percent a year in yield. You probably can double your money in five to six years if the markets treat you right. You also should protect your purchasing power with a position in gold, for you never can be certain when inflation will strike. Gold can earn little or nothing for years, then, in a crisis, while stock and bond prices tumble, shoot up dramatically. In 1973 to 1974, stocks dropped 15 percent overall while gold-mining stocks rose a fantastic 170 percent. For cash reserves, and to cushion the blow of a minor downturn in bonds or stocks, money funds are a choice parking place.

An appropriate mix for you, if you belong to this group, would be 29.5 percent of investable assets in aggressive-stock mutual funds, 9.5 percent in growth and income mutual funds, 1 percent in bond funds, 43 percent in international equity funds, 11 percent in precious-metals mutual funds and 6 percent in a money fund.

Example II. Young professional couple, 30 to 40 years old with one or two children. They want to cut wasteful spending and are willing to take on some risk because they will need $80,000 to pay for their child's (children's) college education in about 16 years.

Much like the couple during the middle adult years, growth is important to these two. They also, however, have immediate and pressing financial commitments. As a result, their risk level shifts lower. Growth is still emphasized; however, the old money-fund account keeps growing larger and larger.

A good mix: 25 percent in aggressive stock funds, 10.5 percent in growth and income mutual funds, 39.5 percent in international mutual funds, 3 percent in bond funds, 9 percent in gold funds, and 11 percent in money-market funds.

Example III. Middle-aged couple of 40 to 50, in their peak earning years. They are saving for retirement, with a child in college, are looking for lower levels of growth and are still seeking protection from inflation. During peak earning years, investors tend to look forward to that swelling retirement fund and the good life lying ahead. You still need growth and inflation protection, but, as you accumulate more wealth, safety of principal becomes a concern.

A good mix: 17.5 percent in growth funds, 5.5 percent in precious-metals funds, 50 percent in money funds and 27 percent in high-grade corporate bonds or bond funds.

Example IV. 50 to 60 years old and getting ready for retirement. They still want growth, but they also want—and need—to protect their money.

A good mix: 13 percent in growth funds, 4 percent in gold funds, 61.5 percent in money funds and 21.5 percent in high-grade corporate bonds or bond funds.

Example V. Retired, over age 60, looking for income and no risk. Most retirees stay with utility stocks because they pay high yields and are considered one of the safest stock-market sectors. (After all, everyone needs electricity.) In addition, senior citizens usually like to play the interest-rate game. They wait for rates to rise and lock into high-yield T-bills and bank accounts.

The big danger for fixed-income investors is watching their purchasing power erode because of inflation. As a result, it is best to invest part of the investment whole in overseas bonds, which often pay higher rates than domestic securities. In addition, foreign bond prices do not move in tandem with ours. You are hedged, because foreign bond prices often outyield domestic bonds. Overseas bonds respond to market conditions in the country of issuance. As a result, bond prices may be rising in Europe when America suffers inflation because European governments control inflation better than America does.

A good mix: 67 percent in certificates of deposit, 8 percent in foreign bonds, 1 percent in money funds and 24 percent in utility stocks.

LADDER YOUR MATURITIES

Laddering the maturities is another safe way to boost your income over certificates of deposit and other money market instruments. A laddered portfolio is a portfolio of bonds maturing at various times, usually in consecutive years. The portfolio earns higher than money market rates. In addition, every year bonds that mature have the chance to be rolled over at high rates. Today, a high quality corporate bond laddered portfolio would yield about 7 percent.

If you have a substantial amount of money considered a laddered portfolio of bonds over a bond fund for a couple of reasons. First, a portfolio can be tailor-made to an investor's time horizon, income stream, and future goals. Second, there are no management fees or annual trustee fees, sales distribution fees or yield enhancements with a customized portfolio compared to an open end bond fund.

Here is an example of a laddered portfolio of bonds. At the time of this writing these high-grade bonds could be stretched out to 7 years: Wachovia 7 percent coupon bond that matures in 12/99; RJR Nabisco 7.625 bond maturing in 09/00; AT&T 7 percent coupon maturing in 02/01; Tampa Electric 7.375 coupon maturing in 01/02; Carolina Power & Light 8.125 coupon maturing in 11/03; and Philip Morris 7.125 coupon maturing in 10/04.

The current yield on the laddered portfolio is 7.28 percent and the investor receives $4,425 in annual income, based on January 6, 1993 prices assuming a $60,000 portfolio.

WATCH THE YIELD CURVE FOR CLUES

No one can predict the direction of interest rates. That's why it's important to watch what the investment pros call the yield curve. Our friend James Benham of the Benham Group of Funds always encourages investors to watch rates for investment signals. When you look at the yield curve, you compare the yield of short-term bonds and T-bills to the yields on long-term Treasury bonds before you invest. For example:

- A positive sloping yield curve. This exists when long-term rates are higher than short-term rates by more than 200 to 250 basis points. Today there is a 400 basis point difference between long- and short-term rates. Under these conditions, Benham suggests investing in the 5-year maturity range. This is the point in the yield curve with the best risk/return trade off.
- A inverted yield curve. This exists when short-term rates are higher than long-term rates. An inverted yield curve existed in the 1980s when short-term rates yielded 16 percent compared to 14 percent in long-term bonds. The curve also inverted in June of 1989 when short-term rates traded at 100 basis points more than long-term rates. An inverted yield curve suggests investors should buy longer-term bonds and profit when interest rates decline later on.
- A humped yield curve. This exists when intermediate term rates are higher than both short- and long-term rates. Investments should be made at the hump, the highest spot in the yield curve. It is considered the safest place on the maturity spectrum.
- A flat yield curve. This exists when there are only slight differences among short-, intermediate-, and long-term rates. Investors should keep up with economic and monetary developments. If the Fed tightens money supply or inflation heats up,

investors should invest short-term because interest rates will rise. By contrast, loose monetary policy favors the long bond.

WHAT TO DO NOW

The yield curve is flattening as we revise the book. Long-term rates are dropping as a result of the Clinton Administration's proposed economic plan. However, as the economy improves, short-term interest rates may rise. So any rise in short-term interest rates would benefit money market fund shareholders quickly and without penalty.

"Long-term bonds are for investing, not saving," says Benham. "Any signs that inflation will pick up, fueled by increased spending by the administration, is likely to force up interest rates. But long rates have come down much less than short-term rates and the margin over inflation is still above historic norms. So the extra risk long-term bondholders encounter is matched by the extra opportunities."

What to do now? Benham advises that you "have enough in money funds to cover all likely needs and some in long-term bonds to get high income and the change for capital appreciation. Then focus on the intermediate range of yields and modest volatility."

AN INFLATION ANTIDOTE

One simple rule of portfolio management dictates always keeping some money in gold- or precious-metals mining stocks as an inflation hedge. We have been experiencing a long period of low inflation, and gold prices have been correspondingly sluggish. Metals mutual funds, for the most part, lag behind diversified equity funds. During periods of high inflation, however, you will be glad that you kept a position in precious metals. According to a study conducted by Lawrence Ritter and

Thomas Urich for the Salomon Brothers Center for the Study of Financial Research in New York, from 1968 through 1983 inflation averaged 7.1 percent a year. Gold registered a real rate of return, or percentage gain less the inflation rate, of nine percent—a whopping eight percent more than stocks earned less inflation and almost 11 percent more than bonds (see Figure 3.1). In addition, they found that when you add a modest position of gold to a portfolio of stocks and bonds, "gold can reduce total portfolio risk [remember our margin of error—it shrinks when you mix in gold] because the rate of return of gold fluctuates opposite to the rate of return on stocks."

Both gold bullion and precious metals funds are volatile investments. Over the past five years ending in

Figure 3.1   U.S. Stocks Versus Foreign Stocks

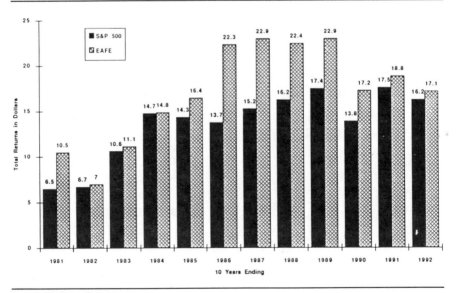

Source: T. Rowe Price

1992 precious metals funds lost −8.75 percent a year. Wham! Clinton is elected, we have an international currency crisis and inflation becomes a concern. At the time we revised the book, precious metals funds gained almost 50 percent.

The lesson: It never hurts to have a little gold in your hip pocket.

THE REAL ESTATE QUESTION

There's an old saying that "If you have to feed it or fix it, don't invest in it." Real estate traditionally has been a good inflation hedge. You should, however, limit this asset in your all-weather portfolio to Real Estate Investment Trusts (REIT) or to the few mutual funds that directly invest in real-estate—related securities. Mutual funds tend to be organized as limited partnerships, a structure that can create problems for investors. Limited partnerships' maturity terms are 15 to 20 years. If you want to sell your units before maturity, you must find a buyer. Data from the National Partnership Exchange reveals that the prices of real-estate limited-partnership units sold on the secondary market dropped steadily in 1988. Based on an index of partnership secondary-market prices, all-cash partnerships that buy property and collect rents lost almost ten percent. Leveraged deals, those that borrow to buy property, declined almost 25 percent during the past year.

Limited partnerships lack too much liquidity to be wise choices for most investors. It makes more sense to invest in a corporation with vast real-estate holdings. Because large corporations typically hold a large share of their assets in the forms of real estate, the common stocks in a well-diversified portfolio are, in fact, indirect real-estate investments.

REITs

If you want to diversify using real estate, it's best to invest in Real Estate Investment Trusts (REITs) or mutual funds that invest in real-estate–related securities. Traditionally, real estate has returned three percent above the inflation rate over the past several decades. With a REIT, you have a liquid inflation hedge in the real-estate market. REITs are securities that are traded on the major stock exchanges. REIT companies own property or make mortgage loans, and investors collect dividends from rent or loan interest. REITs are liquid because the securities can be bought or sold in the stock market, just like those of any other company. You are not locked in to a partnership agreement.

REITs also handily diversify a fixed-income portfolio with property-generated income, along with providing an inflation hedge. Rents usually rise along with inflation; thus, the purchasing power of the income is kept intact. REITs, therefore, have a low correlation with government bonds. You can boost your return without taking on any extra risk. Today an investor could expect to earn 6.5 percent with a margin error of 9.1 percent from a 50/50 split of long-term government bonds and equity REITs. Long-term government bonds alone have an expected return of about 4.7 percent with a margin of error of 11.1 percent.

MUTUAL FUNDS THINK FOR YOU

There are now five mutual funds on the market that invest in REITs and the securities of real estate industries. The funds now yield around 3 percent and have appreciated handsomely over the past couple of years. The Fidelity Real Estate Investment Fund is the best performing fund over the past five years. Over the past five years ended in May of 1993, the fund grew at a 14.2

Table 3.4   Real Rates of Return

Asset	Return	Minus Inflation	Equals	Real Rate of Return
Gold	16.1%	7.1%		9.0%
Silver	10.2	7.1		3.1
Stocks	8.1	7.1		1.0
Housing	8.0	7.1		.9
T-bills	7.5	7.1		.4
Bonds	5.3	7.1		−1.8

Source: Salomon Brothers

---

percent annual rate. Over the last twelve months the fund gained a whopping 24 percent.

Other funds which have performed well over the past three years ended in May 1993 include: PRA Real Estate Securities, up 10 percent annually; Templeton Real Estate Securities, up 12.5 percent annually; and US Real Estate Fund, up 11 percent annually.

A FINANCIAL BOILERMAKER

Mixing a higher-risk investment, such as growth stocks, with risk-free money funds or T-bills gives your investment portfolio a smoother flavor. T-bills, the U.S. government's short-term debt obligations, offer maturities ranging from 3 to 12 months. Money funds are mutual funds that pool investors' money and buy cash instruments: T-bills, bank time deposits and other short-term IOUs. Money-market investments are not volatile: They provide a lower but steadier return. By salting away some assets in T-bills or money funds, you cut down on the price volatility of your portfolio. You essentially dilute the strength of your riskier investments to make your portfolio more palatable. In addition, the income your earn from your money-market investment acts as a cushion against stock losses.

THE STOCK-BOND SEESAW

Bonds, like money-market assets, act as a hedge for stocks. Bonds are long-term IOUs issued by corporations or the U.S. Treasury. They pay higher yields than money funds, but they also are riskier. Bond prices move in opposite directions to interest rates: When interest rates rise, bond prices decline. Conversely, when rates decline, bond prices rally.

Sometimes bond prices rally when stock prices fall, as investors panic and switch their funds from the stock market to safe investments such as Treasury Securities or AAA-rated bonds. Increased demand drives up bond prices. If you own bonds when the stock market falls, the increase in bond value offsets the losses in stocks. Also consider investing in overseas bond funds, which often have different cycles from ours, thus providing another hedge.

SAFETY IN TREASURY BONDS

Examine what happened to mutual funds during the week of October 22, 1987, to October 29, 1987, and you will see how bond-market positions counteract stock-market losses. According to Lipper Analytical Services in New York, small-company growth stocks dropped 9 percent in value in one week, aggressive-stock funds lost 4.7 percent and international-stock funds declined a whopping 11 percent. Bond funds that invested in U.S. Treasury and government agency securities, however, gained almost one percent during the same period, which may not be quite so dramatic, but when the market is plummeting such gains offer welcome relief.

INVESTING OVERSEAS

Once your hedges are in place, you can invest in stocks with confidence. Within the stock pantheon, there are further possible subdivisions. Overseas stocks move a little differently than domestic stocks, and their returns recently have been better. Foreign stocks afford you another hedging option, with good appreciation potential. When you combine undervalued small-company stocks and larger blue-chip stocks with overseas stocks, you earn a better return for your risk.

Figures 3.1 and 3.2, showing the returns on U.S. and overseas securities over the past several years, demonstrate how the extra diversification works. For example, in 1989 foreign bonds lost about 3 percent, while U.S. bonds gain closed to 15 percent. But look what happened in 1987—U.S. bonds grew just 2 percent, compared to a 35 percent gain in foreign bonds. More

---

Figure 3.2   **U.S. Bond Market Versus International Bond Market**

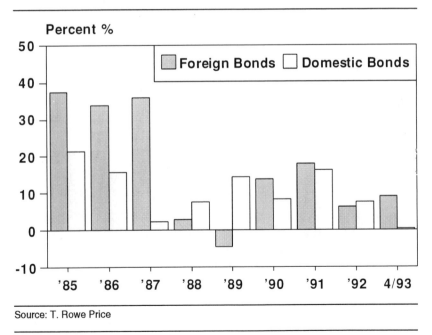

Source: T. Rowe Price

---

recently overseas bonds are outperforming U.S. bonds. Year-to-date ended in April of 1993, overseas bonds are up 10 percent, while U.S. bonds were barely up in value.

Or look at U.S. versus foreign stocks. Figure 3.1 shows that for every ten-year period ending in 1981 through 1992, foreign stocks have outperformed U.S. equities. Year by year U.S. and overseas stocks take turns besting each other's returns. What's important is that most of the time, gains overseas will offset losses or low returns here at home.

A WIDER INVESTMENT CHOICE

The U.S. bond and stock markets represent only about one-third of the world's markets. Europe, Australia, and the Far East constitute the rest. In these often exotic ports of call, investors can find overlooked opportunities.

A report published in 1988 by the New York investment banking firm Morgan Stanley & Co. documented the fact that worldwide markets offer better value than U.S. domestic markets. Morgan Stanley found several overseas securities underpriced based on future earnings expectation. As a result, international stocks probably will outperform the S&P 500 and many of the U.S. domestic equity-fund portfolio managers.

TOP PERFORMERS OVERSEAS

The Morgan Stanley & Co. report of a few years ago was on target. Since 1988 overseas mutual funds have lived up to their expectations. Their performance leads and lags behind domestic equity funds. This makes overseas funds good candidates for a diversified portfolio of mutual funds. Over the past ten years ending in April 1993, international stock funds grew at an annual rate of 13.09 percent, compared to the 11.25 annual return on the average U.S. stock fund. U.S. funds grew at an annual rate of 13.53 percent and outpaced international funds by 8 percentage points of annual return over the past five years. This year-to-date, the returns are again reversed. International funds gained 13.75 percent, while U.S. funds are up just 3.36 percent.

NO PAIN, NO GAIN

Investing overseas, of course, is not painless. One-third of the price appreciation in overseas stock markets is because of the drop in the dollar, according to Morgan Stanley. Foreign currencies strengthen when the dollar declines, and stocks purchased in other currencies appreciate. Naturally, the pendulum swings both ways. If the dollar increases in value, foreign stock prices will decline.

FOREIGN BONDS

Overseas bonds also can play a part in a diversified portfolio. Research has shown that, worldwide, fixed-income securities lead and lag, playing off one another. Discrepancies exist in yields and currency values, so international bond funds can work as a hedge against falling U.S. bond prices.

Salomon Brothers' research describes the foreign bond markets as deep and highly liquid, making up 50 percent of the world bond arena. With this liquidity, there is a readily available market for overseas bonds of European and Asian issuers, and they can be sold quickly.

Foreign bonds also have outperformed U.S. bonds over a number of holding periods. Since 1960, foreign-bond portfolios have shown an average total return of 8.2 percent for ten-year periods, compared to 5.9 percent for U.S. bonds. At the same time, the two markets have differed little in price volatility.

Another plus is that only a low correlation exists between U.S. and foreign bonds. According to Ibbotson Associates, a number of bonds issued by foreign countries had negative or low correlation with U.S. Government bonds.

Adding foreign bonds to a fixed-income portfolio can reduce volatility. A mix of 60/40 U.S. and foreign bonds will be almost half as volatile as a 100 percent position in the U.S. bonds.

STILL NO FREE LUNCH

Foreign bonds or bond funds come equipped with their own set of risks. If foreign currencies weaken against the dollar, the market value of the bonds will decline. In the event of a bond-market disaster, worldwide markets could decline together. In the past, from 1965 through mid-1966, according to Federal Reserve Bank of St. Louis data, U.S., U.K., Swiss, and German long-term interest rates peaked together before declining. The same thing happened in 1970 and 1974, while rates seemed to bottom out in all of those countries between 1977 and 1978 before rising.

MIX AND MATCH

Later chapters will determine the best mix for you, based on your own comfort level. You *can* create your own portfolio mix, based on your tolerance for risk. If you want growth, shift more money into the volatile but lucrative area of stocks. More moderate investors can split up the pie equally. The more conservative you are, the more money you put in T-bills or money funds.

What counts is the mix: getting and keeping the right investment formula. As in fine baking, if you put in the right amount of quality ingredients, you will be satisfied with the results.

PART
2

Building Your Portfolio

CHAPTER 4

Individual Securities

If you are a do-it-yourself investor who likes to make his or her own investment decisions, then you can put together your own asset-allocation portfolio. To allocate your portfolio yourself, you will need at least $50,000 to $100,000, so you can buy enough different types of securities to ensure diversification.

Previous chapters explained risk levels, and how to split up your investments to match your risk level. Low-risk investors would heavily weight their portfolios with money funds, then split up their remaining funds among bonds, growth, and income stocks. Once you have the proper mix, you evaluate performance at least quarterly, and if your risk level or financial condition changes, you reset your formula.

This chapter will review the basics of investing in stocks and bonds and how to pick securities and also will provide you with a list of recommended securities.

61

TAKE A LONG-TERM APPROACH

A good stockbroker will tell you to select stocks that meet your risk level and investment goals, and then to invest for the long term. When you pick up *The Wall Street Journal* and read the column entitled "Abreast of the Market," however, all you learn is how daily economic events affect stock prices. You also may read that a large volume of trades that day sent stock prices tumbling.

About 140 to 200 million shares are traded every day on the New York Stock Exchange. Who is doing all that buying and selling, if brokerage firms tell clients that wise investors buy and hold? Actually, the institutional investors react most to daily events in the market. The category of institutional investors includes the brokerage firms themselves, pension funds, insurance companies and mutual funds; these provide three-fourths of the frenetic activity on the exchanges. Individual investors account for only about 25 percent of the trading volume in the financial markets.

Is the deck stacked against you? Not as long as you buy undervalued stocks—stocks with prices that do not reflect current and potential earnings. If you buy low, you can become the seller when the institutional investors turn their restless attention to your stock.

News about interest rates, inflation and the trade and budget deficits is irrelevant on a day-to-day basis. During the next five and ten years, growth companies will continue to profit and reward shareholders with increasing dividends and stock-price gains. Public utilities will continue to pay handsome dividends. Regardless of market movements, companies in fad industries will eventually falter, and their stock prices will tumble. Remember what happened to Coleco, the marketers of that puffy-faced doll called the Cabbage Patch Kid. Coleco's stock soared to more than 200 percent in the early 1980s. After consumers had their fill of these strange-looking toys, though, the price of Coleco stock tumbled drastically. Many investors who bought in at the end of the upward spiral lost large amounts of money.

Consequently, you should not place too much emphasis on monthly economic statistics when you make investment decisions. Asset-allocation decisions should be made on the basis of what return you want in relation to how much risk you are willing to take. Stock selection should be made on the basis of what the investment pros call fundamentals. Is the stock's price undervalued in relation to its future earnings? Is the stock's price a bargain compared with the book value of the firm or the price per share the investor would receive if the company were liquidated and the assets sold? Is the stock overlooked now by institutional investors and analysts who can be counted on to buy sooner or later as long as the stock's numbers remain attractive?

What should you do today? Let's start by contemplating a few numbers. Common stocks with normal risk values have provided investors with an average annual return of ten percent over the past six decades. Intermediate-term Treasury bonds currently yield 6.5 percent, while money funds yield 3 percent. With that combination of returns on your side, you have the makings of a strong allocated portfolio.

Most importantly, you should seek reasonable value when you buy common stocks—which means buying stocks with prices that do not reflect the earnings potential of the company or buying higher dividend-yielding blue-chip stocks that are underpriced.

Many of today's real values can be found in growth companies traded on the over-the-counter stock market. These less-capitalized companies often sport annual growth rates of 15 percent and sell for 12 to 14 times their previous year's earnings. In addition, the earnings of many of these companies tend to be recession-resistant. Large companies usually contract during recessions, while growth companies often create new products and expand their market share, unless a recession is severe and prolonged.

IS THE STOCK MARKET RIGGED?

Concerns about the Wall Street "Big Boys" moving in and out of a large volume of stock based on computer information has caused many to stay away from investing. The evidence suggests that the stock market is rigged. But it's rigged in our favor. It's rigged in favor of the true investor who makes a long-term commitment to common stock investing. It's rigged in favor of those investors who assume no more risk than they can comfortably tolerate and maintain a well-diversified portfolio.

ONE STEP BACK, THEN TWO STEPS FORWARD

The financial data shows that people who invest for the long term and diversify can take advantage of the volatility in the stock market to meet their financial goals and objectives. For example, if you look at the total returns on the S&P 500 from 1926–1992 (see Table 4.1) and use different trading strategies, you can see that the longer you stay in the market, the better chances you have of making money.

Investors who bought and sold the S&P 500 annually profited during 66 years and lost money during 19 years. The investor who maintained a diversified portfolio of average risk, as represented by the S&P 500, would have lost money 30.6 percent of the time. This means that you can expect to give up three yards on the investment football field, then pick up six yards on the ensuing drive to the goal line. You make one step back and two steps forward.

STOCKS BEAT T-BILLS HANDS DOWN

If you compare long-term stock investors' returns to Treasury-bill investors' returns, the stock-market investor is the big winner 61.3 percent of the time. The largest annual gain one could have made in stocks was 54 percent during 1933. The biggest loss was 43.3 percent in 1931. The median or middle annual return in stocks during this 62-year period was 13.4 percent. The T-bill investor who likes to play it safe would have never experienced a loss during this 62-year period. The largest annual gain was 14.7 percent in 1981. The median return over 62 years was three percent.

Table 4.1   Common Stock versus Treasury Bill Returns Various Holding Periods 1926 to Present

Holding Period (Years)	1	5	10	15
Common Stocks (S&P 500)				
Largest Loss	−43.3%	−48.9%	−8.8%	Gain
Largest Gain	54.0	191.9	491.0	1125.4
Median Annual Return	13.4	10.8	9.2	9.8
Probability of Loss	30.6	13.8	3.8	0.0
Probability Return Greater than T-Bill Return	61.3	77.6	81.1	91.7
Treasury Bills				
Smallest Gain	0.0	0.5	1.0	2.9
Largest Gain	14.7	68.3	125.7	223.4
Median Annual Return	3.0	2.5	2.1	2.1

Source: Investment Information Services

THE LONGER YOU HOLD STOCKS, THE LESS YOU MAY LOSE

If these statistics are representative of future investment returns, then the individual who holds on to stocks for an average of one year stands to profit nearly two-thirds of the time. The longer you hold on to stocks, however, the greater your chance of making money increases. Consider what happens when you hold on for 5, 10, and 15 years. If you held stocks for one year, your largest loss during the period from 1926 through 1987 would have been 43.3 percent. Over a five-year holding period, the largest loss would have been 48.9 percent. But if you held for ten years, the largest loss would have been 8.8 percent. Over 15-year holding periods there were no losing periods in the past 62 years.

OVER THE SHORT TERM YOU CAN PICK UP BIGGER GAINS

You also can see from this table that the shorter the holding period, the larger the average gain. Over one year you would have earned a 13.4 percent gain. This return drops to 9.8 percent for 15-year holding periods. Obviously, the probability of loss decreases the longer you hold on to your investment. For one-year holding periods you run about a 31-percent chance of losing money. The probability of loss over 5-, 10-, and 15-year holding periods drops significantly to 13.8 percent, 3.8 percent and 0, respectively.

THE LONGER YOU HOLD STOCKS, THE MORE YOU OUTPERFORM T-BILLS

In addition, the longer you hold on to stocks, the greater the chance you have of outperforming T-bills. You have a 61.23 percent chance of beating T-bills with a one-year holding period and a 91.7 percent chance of coming out on top, if you hold stocks for 15 years.

66

THE LONGER THE HOLDING PERIOD, THE LOWER THE ANNUAL LOSS

Some investment advisors scoff at buying and holding for the long haul. They claim that they can make judgments by using computer-driven buy-and-sell programs, which are based on economic and stock market price trends, to move in and out of the markets to maximize gains. These advisors may be right for a short period of time, but over the long term market timers fail to beat the market averages over the long term.

When you hold stocks for the long term, you always are fully invested to catch the turns in the market. You might take one step back as mentioned previously, but when you are in position to catch a rebound with all your money, you make two steps forward. For example, Table 4.2 shows the annual losses for 5-, 10-, and 15-year holding periods. During these times, the longer you hold on, the less money you will lose. The maximum loss you would have experienced for five years from 1928 to 1932 was an annual –12.5 percent. For ten years from 1929 to 1938 you would have lost –.9 percent and for 15 years from 1929 to 1943 you would have gained .6 percent annually.

THE MORE YOU INVEST A YEAR, THE BIGGER YOUR GAIN

Not only do you reduce the risk of loss the longer you hold on, but you can profit by making annual investments. You can buy shares at a lower price during down years and when the market rebounds, the average cost is below the market price. For example, if you invested $1,000 for the 5-, 10-, and 15-year holding periods, you would have amassed $2,710 after five years. You lost some money, but for ten years the $10,000 invested was worth $14,807. In 15 years, even during the maximum loss period, the $15,000 invested was worth $24,558. As you can see, that's a lot more than a T-bill investment.

Table 4.2   Spotlight on Maximum Loss Periods

	5-year	10-year	15-year
Common Stocks (S&P 500)			
Annual Loss	−12.5%	−0.9%	gain 0.6%
Years	1928-32	1929-38	1929-43
Buy and Hold ($1,000)	$511	$912	$1,091
Invest $1,000 each year	$2,701	$14,807	$24,558
Treasury Bills			
Buy and Hold ($1,000)	$1,129	$1,105	$1,112
Invest $1,000 each year	$5,301	$10,258	$15,360

Source: Investment Information Services

BACK TO BASICS

Let's take a step backward now and look specifically at stocks and bonds and how you should choose them. Later on in the chapter, we will list some stocks for you to consider. You also can obtain brokerage-firm reports and find out what stocks the analysts think are undervalued and what bonds they are currently recommending.

YOU'RE AN OWNER IN THE COMPANY WHEN YOU BUY STOCK

When you buy a share or shares of stock in a corporation, you become a partial owner of the company. This ownership position enables you to share in the growth of the firm and of the economy by seeing your stock price and dividend payments rise over time. As the economy grows, so do the earnings of corporations. According to data published by Ibbotson Associates of Chicago, over the past 60 years small-company growth stocks have risen at an annual rate of 12 percent—and larger stocks at an annual 10 percent. Compare these to 8 percent for corporate bonds, 4 percent for T-bills, and 4.3 percent for the rate of inflation.

LONG-TERM GAINS AND SHORT-TERM SWINGS

Over the short term, stock prices can be volatile. Stock prices swing because of changes in interest rates, political events and changes in the economy, government economic policy, and investor expectations.

In the long run, however, stock prices represent past, present and future growth in corporate earnings. According to Standard & Poor's data, for example, corporate earnings in dollars per share have increased from $4 per share to $24 per share from 1949 through the end of decade of the 1980s. At the same time annual dividends have grown from about $2 to about $10 per share. In the 1990s, it looks like this trend will continue because the earnings on S&P 500 stocks are growing at a 22 percent annual rate. Share price can fluctuate daily, monthly, or even annually. If you have a long-term investment outlook, your gains eventually will outpace your setbacks. The longer you hold on to your investments, the more you reduce your risk of loss.

DO YOUR HOMEWORK

You must do a certain amount of homework when you invest in individual stocks. A stock's price is influenced by economic events—events that pertain to an individual company or its industry. This is why it is important to diversify and invest in a number of securities in different industries.

IS A STOCK UNDERVALUED OR OVERVALUED?

There are numerous ways to evaluate stocks. One of the most important variables is a company's price-to-earnings ratio (p/e), which is calculated by dividing the stock price by its earnings per share. This figure will provide you with an idea of how the market values this stock. A high p/e may be good if the company has a record of profitability and growth—perhaps it reflects market expectations that corporate earnings will increase. If the firm's earnings are too low, however, the high p/e may indicate that the stock is very overpriced. Conversely, a lower p/e may indicate that a stock is undervalued—if the price is low in relation to the company's current and expected future earnings.

Since 1926, the p/e ratio of the Standard & Poor's 500 stock index has averaged 13.7 percent. You can use this average as a benchmark to evaluate stocks. You also must compare the p/e ratio of a firm you are interested in with those of its peers. This information you can obtain from your stockbroker or by using the Value Line Investment Survey and Standard & Poor's reports.

ASSESS THE FIRM'S FINANCIAL STRENGTH

In addition to value, you must consider a company's financial condition and management ability. Several measurements can help you assess financial strength. All the information you will need is available in company annual and quarterly reports and brokerage-firm reports. You should look at several years' worth of data on the firm and compare its performance with that of its competitors.

Three salient financial statements are listed in a firm's annual report. The income statement lists the firm's revenues, expenses, taxes paid, and net earnings. The balance sheet lists the firm's liquid assets, long-term assets and total assets, as well as current liabilities, long-term debts, stockholders' equity and total liabilities and equity. The

Sources and Uses of Funds statement provides the company's sources of funds and how those funds were used.

Several important measurements to consider when analyzing a firm's annual and quarterly financial statements are as follows:

- *Return on Equity*. This calculation tells how well the company is being managed—what kind of rate of return you are receiving on your ownership. To arrive at this figure, divide the net earnings of the company (listed in the firm's income statement) by the average equity value of stock ownership or net worth of the firm, listed in the balance sheet for the year.
- *Operating-Profit Margin*. To determine this measurement from the firm's income statement, just divide operating profits by sales. This figure shows how profitable it is for your company to produce its product.
- *Net-Profit Margin*. This margin shows how profitable a firm is after meeting all of its expenses. On the income statement, divide the net earnings by the total revenue.
- *Current Ratio*. This figure indicates financial strength. Look at the balance sheet and divide assets by current liabilities.
- *Capitalization*. Capitalization is how much debt a firm carries, from issuing bonds and borrowing money, in relation to its stockholder equity. This information is available from the balance sheet. Conservatively managed companies will have a low level of debt in relation to equity. More aggressively managed companies borrow more money through loans and the bond market than by selling stock.
- *Cash Flow*. This number shows how much money the firm has available to allocate to new-product development, plant, and equipment. If a firm has a strong cash flow as compared to its competitors, it can

engage in new activities or increase production without having to borrow money or issue new bonds or stock. Cash flow equals net income plus depreciation.

- *Earnings per Share.* This figure indicates how profitable the company is in terms of its outstanding stock. To calculate this figure, divide the net earnings by the number of shares outstanding.

HOW TO PICK GROWTH STOCKS

Unless you are retired and living on a fixed income, you must have a growth component in your diversified portfolio, even if it is as little as ten percent. An excellent way to zip up the return on your allocated portfolio is to buy small-company growth stocks. They are risky and volatile, but not when you temper your investment with bonds, cash, and inflation hedges such as gold. Small stocks have grown at an annual rate of 12 percent over the past 60 years, with some stomach-churning price swings of 20 percent or more a year. Over the long term, a well-selected portfolio of growth stocks will be a lucrative investment.

WHAT IS A GROWTH FIRM?

A growth firm is a company with sales, earnings, dividends, and stock prices that are expected to grow faster than the normal rate. Normal growth would be a three-to five-percent annual increase in earnings and stock price above the contemporaneous rate of inflation. A growth stock should grow at least ten percent annually.

STAGES OF CORPORATE GROWTH

Stage I is the embryonic phase.   Figure 4.1 shows the typical life cycle of a company, which usually begins with the invention of a new product or service. Because

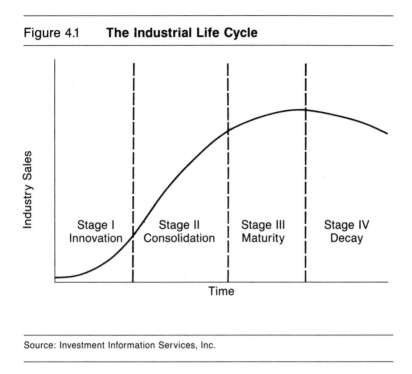

Figure 4.1   **The Industrial Life Cycle**

Source: Investment Information Services, Inc.

this product or service presumably appears in response to an unfilled demand in the marketplace, the product will appear to be in high demand. Once other entrepreneurs see the new product's success, however, they may copycat the firm and duplicate its business. All these upstarts will have one thing in common—they will need money. Capital, raised by selling stock to the public, keeps the production lines running to meet demand and outpace competition.

Several other characteristics typify start-up companies. New firms may need to use all of their capital to strengthen their business. Management, therefore, will pump earnings back into the firm rather than pay out part of its profits to shareholders in the form of stock dividends. Lack of dividends is one disadvantage growth companies hold for investors. Another is the company's greater instability at this period of corporate life, because of management inexperience, excessive competition, high operating costs, and lower profit margins. During this embryonic stage in the business life cycle, bankruptcy is a much more imminent possibility.

During this stage, however, the common stock of firms with positive earnings per share of stock is positive. For this reason, many investors are optimistic about the outlook for the firm. The stock price is driven up and the price per share of the stock in relation to its earnings per share, or p/e ratio, is extremely high. This p/e ratio is like a thermometer for it reflects the expectations of future profitability and indicates value. If a firm has strong earnings, for example, but the price of the stock is lower than it should be, the p/e ratio indicates that the stock is a bargain. Conversely, if the p/e ratio is high, but not excessively high compared to other stocks in the same industry group, this could indicate that the stock price might go higher because investors see earnings on the move. When the p/e ratio is at extremes, however, either too high or too low relative to the overall stock-market and peer-group stocks, this indicates that the stock is overpriced or is a real loser.

Stage II is the consolidation phase. During this phase of the corporate life cycle, the wheat is separated from the chaff—the industry experiences a natural shakeout and a number of firms go out of business. The most-competitive and well-managed companies will survive, but many cannot maintain quality output or sufficient volume or simply cannot raise enough capital to expand.

The consolidation phase also is characterized by a slowdown in the growth of sales to an annual rate of perhaps 15 percent, down from a start-up level of 40 percent. Those firms that survive will have gained much-needed management experience, production, and product-distribution efficiency to offset the tempering of their sales increases.

Shareholders in surviving companies begin to reap the benefits of their investment. These growing companies may start paying out 10 to 30 percent of their earnings in cash dividends. Many firms also issue more stock and use the proceeds to expand their business. Investment risks still exist at this stage, but the potential for the company to continue growing is high and is reflected in price-to-earnings ratios that range from 10 to 40 times that of earnings.

Stage III is the maturity phase. Typical firms in the maturity phase of their lives are companies such as IBM, Exxon, Pfizer, Dow Chemical, Philip Morris, and General Motors—only a handful of large, well-seasoned companies make it to this level. Much of their product demand now consists of replacement demand, so sales and earnings growth slows to a rate that parallels the U.S. economic growth rate. The need for new capital also declines and the firms may pay as much as 50 percent of earnings in dividends. Institutional investors such as mutual funds, pension funds, and insurance companies tend to be major shareholders in mature firms and the investment risks are moderately low. The price-to-earnings ratios of these firms fall from the highs of the consolidation phase to multiples of five to ten times that of earnings.

Stage IV is the decay phase. During this stage the demand for output declines and the firms begin to liquidate or sell off their production facilities. Firms with competent management can avoid this phase by acquiring businesses at the consolidation stage and replacing their own older product lines.

WHEN TO INVEST

Understanding what stage in the growth cycle companies are at can be valuable for investors. From an investing standpoint, the best time to invest in a company for long-term profit is during its consolidation stage. Profits also are possible with start-up firms, but mortality rates are high and risk is commensurate. Investing during the consolidation phase also is risky, but less so, and returns can average 18 percent per share over the long term.

Investing in firms at this stage means paying higher-than-average price-to-earnings ratios, between 10 and 30 times that of earnings. This also means going without high-dividend yields, which tend to cushion stock-price declines. Small firms—and these are small, with equity capitalization or the market value of outstanding stock at less than $100 million—have not yet attracted the attention of institutional investors, who dominate the stock market and thus bid up prices. Institutions generally hold less than 15 percent of the outstanding shares of these firms.

WHAT SHOULD YOU PAY FOR GROWTH STOCK?

Growth stocks are characterized by high and fluctuating p/e ratios. In the earlier stages of growth, p/e ratios are lofty. As growth slows, p/e ratios tend to fall. How much should you pay for corporate growth?

Some investors only acquire common shares when they trade at very low p/e multiples. If one firm is selling at a lower p/e multiple than another one, however, this does not necessarily indicate that the firm with the lower p/e represents the greater bargain. For example, suppose two firms, A and B, each report per-share earnings of $1 during 1985 (see Table 4.3). Also assume that the firms have equivalent risk. The common stock of A is priced at $8 and is trading at a p/e multiple of eight times last year's earnings per share, while firm B's common stock is priced at $10 and carries a p/e of ten.

Also assume that over the next five years, firm A grows at a ten-percent annual compound rate, while firm B grows by 20 percent a year. After five years, the future growth rates of both firms will be equal and, at this time, both firms will sell at a p/e multiple of eight times current earnings.

Table 4.3 Comparison of Future Growth Rates

Year	Earnings per share A	Earnings per share B
1985	$1.00	$1.00
1986	1.10	1.20
1987	1.21	1.44
1988	1.32	1.73
1989	1.45	2.07
1990	1.60	2.49

After five years of growth at ten percent annually, the earnings per share of firm A in 1990 are $1.60 and the earnings of B, which grew at 20 percent, are $2.49. Because the shares of both firms now are priced at eight times earnings, the shares of firm A would be worth $12.80 (8 × $1.60) and the shares of B would be $19.92 (8 × $2.49). Over this five-year period, an investor would have earned a 60 percent return with firm A, representing an increase from $8.00 to $12.80 per share. An investment in firm B, however, would have gained almost 100 percent.

The shares of firm B, which had a higher p/e ratio than firm A had, represent the real investment bargain. If an investor, however, paid $15 to acquire shares of firm B in 1989—paying 15 times current earnings instead of ten times earnings—the total investment return over the five years would have been slightly less than 50 percent. Firm A, therefore, with a price-to-earnings multiple of eight times current earnings, would have been a better buy.

Over the past 60 years, stocks with average risks have grown at an annual compound rate of ten percent, composed of three percent dividend yield and seven percent stock-price appreciation. Investors in a typical stock with typical growth prospects should earn a rate of return close to this average.

Investors in growth-company stocks should receive and require a higher-than-average return on their investment as compensation for assuming higher risks. Just how much more is a difficult number to determine. Considering the long-term rates of return earned by successful money managers, however, we learn that they look for an average annual return of 15 to 20 percent on their portfolios of growth stock.

Let's assume that it is possible to earn an 18 percent annual average return on carefully chosen growth stocks. At that rate, your money would double every four years and, after 30 years, a $1 investment would have increased to $143.40.

Table 4.4 lists the maximum price-to-earnings multiples that will yield an 18 percent annual return on common stocks of firms with varying projected growth rates and current dividend yields. The price-to-earnings multiples were obtained by assuming that the indicated growth rate will persist for 12 years and at the end of that time will slow to approximate that of the U.S. economy. The shares of these common stocks would, at that slowdown point, be priced at ten times current earnings, which is the average price-to-earnings multiple of the overall stock market.

Using these assumptions, earnings per share and stock price were projected 12 years into the future. These prices, along with any cash dividends, were discounted to the present (when the stock price is divided by 18 percent over time, you get its present value) and the p/e ratio was determined by dividing the result by the assumed current level of earnings per share.

If the earnings per share of a nondividend-paying firm are currently $1, for example, that figure will climb to $8.92 after ten years of compound growth at the annual rate of 20 percent. If the growth slows to the normal rate of ten percent, the price-to-earnings multiple would be ten times that of current earnings. The share price 12 years into the future should be 10 multiplied by $8.92 (the p/e multiple multiplied by current earnings per share) or $89.20.

Table 4.4   Estimated Earnings Growth

Maximum p/e ratios that will provide an 18 percent compound annual rate-of-investment return for various combinations of current yield and earnings growth.

Current Dividend Yield	Estimated Earnings Growth					
	5%	10%	15%	20%	25%	30%
0%	3	4	7	12	20	32
1%	3	5	8	14	22	35
2%	3	5	9	15	24	39
3%	3	6	10	17	27	44
4%	4	7	11	19	30	49
5%	4	7	12	21	34	54
6%	5	8	14	23	37	60
7%	5	9	15	26	42	67
8%	6	10	17	29	46	74

Source: Investment Information Services, Inc.

To evaluate growth companies using the data from these complicated assumptions, look at Table 4.5. First, you must estimate the long-run growth prospects of the firm and obtain its current dividend yield. Locate these values on the table and find the point at which the appropriate row and column intersect. The value at the intersection point represents the maximum price-to-earnings multiple that should be paid for that company's stock. At or below this level, investors will experience earnings potential of 18 percent annually over the long term.

For instance, you have been watching an attractive growth company in its consolidation phase and its stock is paying a dividend of two percent. You have read reports that agree that the firm's earnings should grow at 15 percent a year. Considering these particulars, you will know that you should not buy the stock if the p/e ratio is nine or above.

This p/e multiple also can be applied to next year's earnings-per-share estimate. For example, a firm is expected to grow at 25 percent a year, paying no dividends. Investors can claim their 18 percent annual (long-term) potential if they pay no more than 20 times the earnings for the stock. If the firm is paying a dividend of two percent times next year's estimated earnings, you should not pay more than 24 times those earnings to retain sufficient return potential—18 percent—to justify your risk.

You also can use this table to choose high-yield common stocks. If you are considering a utility stock that yields eight percent and is expected to grow at ten percent a year, you should not pay more than ten times the earnings to retain the 18-percent horizon.

We have discussed at length how to buy growth stocks on value. It is important to understand the reasons why the price of the stock in relation to its earnings is or is not considered in a buying range. For the sake of convenience, however, you can just use the table to find the appropriate p/e ratio to use to buy stocks.

Using this system should not be a passive endeavor. You as an investor must do the necessary homework to make the system work. Developing a feel for the stock market's activity by keeping up with business news can become your greatest asset. You will want to know what firms are outpacing their competition, what different firms' managements are doing, how companies are marketing their products and how much they are spending on research and development.

Keep up with the business press. *Business Week, Barron's* and *The Wall Street Journal* are invaluable sources of current commercial and economic news; if you do not subscribe to them, consider checking these periodicals regularly in a local library. Also consider subscribing to a few growth-stock newsletters. Ask your broker for copies of analysts' reports, which estimate a company's growth potential and future earnings per share. Once you have compiled this information, you can check the p/e ratio of a stock based on current earnings and compare it to what is listed in Table 4.5. If all of the investment criteria look good, consider buying, but remember to consider each individual purchase in terms of maintaining a diversified portfolio.

At the time of this writing, the information in Table 4.5 indicates attractive growth stocks worth considering. (Information on these stocks was published in *Investment Horizons,* produced by the Investment Information Services in Chicago.) These stocks meet the criteria discussed previously.

BALANCING YOUR GROWTH-STOCK PORTFOLIO

It is vital to stress the importance of asset allocation. Investors who want to temper their risks may want to balance their portfolio with growth and income and overseas stocks, as well as with precious metals as an inflation hedge. Earlier in the book we discussed several investment mixes you could use to boost your return while adding the least possible risk to your portfolio.

For example, low-risk investors who want to participate in the upward mobility of the small stock market could mellow their risks by placing 4 percent of their portfolio in aggressive stocks, 10 percent in growth and income blue-chip stocks, 17 percent in foreign stocks, 4 percent in precious metals and 65 percent in a money fund, which would be a facsimile of the safety and yield of a Treasury bill. With that kind of mix, you could expect an annual return of 11.7 percent with a margin of error of 7.4 percent on either side.

Table 4.5   Growth Stocks to Buy

Current Recommendations

Company (Industry)	Exchange	Ticker Symbol	Recent Price	52-Week High	52-Week Low	Advice	Sales (mil.)	5-Year Sales Growth	12-Mo. EPS
AEP Industries *(Plastics)*	OTC	AEPI	$16 1/4	$17 3/4	$ 9 3/4	Buy	$149.3	13%	$0.93
Aceto *(Chemicals)*	OTC	ACET	14 1/4	17 1/2	12 5/8	Buy	157.9	8	0.35
Alcide *(Disinfectants)*	OTC	ALCD	9 1/2	10 3/4	4 1/4	Buy	6.5	30	0.50
Analysts Int'l *(Software/Consulting)*	OTC	ANLY	31	35 3/4	16 1/4	Buy	154.7	18	1.57
Andros, Inc. *(Analysis Equipment)*	OTC	ANDY	15 7/8	19 1/4	10 7/8	Buy	31.0	21	0.92
Artistic Greetings *(Stationery Products)*	OTC	ARTG	5 1/2	11 1/2	5 1/4	Buy	75.9	49	0.32
Bio-Rad Labs *(Health/Science Mfr.)*	AMEX	BIOA	14 3/8	20	13 3/8	Buy	327.2	16	1.02
Boston Acoustics *(Loudspeakers)*	OTC	BOSA	15 3/4	20 3/4	12 3/4	Buy	33.0	14	1.12
Central Sprinkler *(Sprinklers)*	OTC	CNSP	11	13	7	Buy	70.5	3	0.20
CONMED *(Hospital Products)*	OTC	CNMD	12	23 1/2	7	Buy	41.8	32	0.53
Cosmetic Center *(Retail Cosmetics)*	OTC	COSCA	15 1/4	16	10 3/4	Buy	106.6	17	0.78
Dixie Yarns *(Textiles)*	OTC	DXYN	11 1/4	16 3/4	9 1/4	Buy	509.3	-5	0.75
EMCON Associates *(Env/Engineering)*	OTC	MCON	6 3/4	12 1/2	5 1/2	Buy	80.5	36	0.35
Ecology & Environment *(Env Testing)*	AMEX	EEI	16 1/8	18 3/8	11 1/4	Buy	76.6	16	1.11
Ecko *(Household Products)*	NYSE	EKO	9 1/2	12 1/8	6 1/2	Buy	206.6	37	0.29
Engraph *(Packaging)*	OTC	ENGH	13	14 1/2	8 1/2	Hold	242.8	17	0.59
Eskimo Pie *(Ice Cream Products)*	OTC	EPIE	18 3/4	23 3/4	14 3/4	Buy	66.2	NM	0.96
Flexsteel Industries *(Furniture)*	OTC	FLXS	16 3/4	17 1/4	10	Buy	173.4	-1	0.69
Frozen Food Exp. *(Perishables Trans.)*	OTC	FFEX	20	20	9 1/8	Buy	207.5	19	0.84
The Future Now *(Comp. Support Svcs.)*	OTC	FNOW	12 1/4	15 1/4	8 1/4	Buy	428.7	NM	1.28
Genovese Drug Stores *(Drugstores)*	AMEX	GDXA	11 1/8	11 1/2	6 3/8	Buy	467.9	8	0.90
Geraghty & Miller *(Env/Engineering)*	OTC	GMGW	9	12 1/2	8 1/2	Buy	137.7	33	0.57
Gish Biomedical *(Hospital Products)*	OTC	GISH	5 1/4	9 7/8	4 3/4	Buy	21.7	17	0.51
GoodMark Foods *(Food)*	OTC	GDMK	16	16 3/4	10 1/2	Buy	141.2	7	1.12
Grist Mill *(Food Mfgr.)*	OTC	GRST	7	14 1/8	7	Buy	66.5	24	0.54
Guardsman Products *(Chemicals)*	NYSE	GPI	13	14	8 3/8	Buy	157.8	2	0.40
Input/Output *(Seismic Technology)*	OTC	IPOP	15 1/2	19 3/4	9 3/4	Buy	54.2	60	1.23
International Jensen *(Loudspeakers)*	OTC	IJIN	8	11 1/4	7 1/4	Buy	201.2	NM	0.97
J & J Snack Foods *(Snack Foods)*	OTC	JJSF	18 1/4	18 1/4	7 1/2	Buy	140.9	20	0.67
Johnson Worldwide *(Recreation Prdct.)*	OTC	JWAIA	21 1/4	22 1/4	14 3/4	Buy	339.8	11	0.92
Keane *(Software Consulting)*	AMEX	KEA	30 3/4	31 1/8	14 7/8	Buy	136.6	18	1.46
Lindsay Mfg. *(Irrigation Systems)*	OTC	LINZ	27	36 1/4	27	Buy	98.5	13	2.22
Marten Transport *(Motor Carrier)*	OTC	MRTN	14 1/4	14 1/2	8	Buy	105.2	11	1.28
Medex *(Hospital Products)*	OTC	MDEX	11 3/4	25 1/2	11 1/8	Buy	92.8	27	0.91
Met-Pro *(Waste Management)*	AMEX	MPR	11 1/2	13 7/8	9 7/8	Buy	37.8	7	0.64
Oil-Dri *(Absorbent Materials)*	OTC	OILC	24 3/4	25	16	Buy	132.2	15	1.36
Osmonics *(Filtration Devices)*	OTC	OSMO	17 1/4	21 1/2	13 1/4	Hold	53.8	18	0.81
Pomeroy *(Computer Support Svcs.)*	OTC	PMRY	7 3/4	8 3/4	4	Buy	87.0	NM	0.51
Puerto Rican Cement *(Cement)*	NYSE	PRN	25 7/8	26 3/4	20 7/8	Buy	81.1	1	1.88
Respironics *(Medical Products)*	OTC	RESP	19 1/2	31	15 1/4	Hold	69.3	37	0.85
S & K Famous Brands *(Retail Clothes)*	OTC	SKFB	20 1/2	22 1/4	7 1/2	Buy	89.2	14	0.79
Sanderson Farms *(Chicken Farmers)*	OTC	SAFM	18 3/4	24 1/2	13 1/2	Buy	232.5	6	1.03
Schult Homes *(Home Builder)*	AMEX	SHC	11 1/2	19 3/8	11	Buy	207.8	10	1.16
Seattle FilmWorks *(Photo Processing)*	OTC	FOTO	16 1/4	16 1/2	9 3/4	Buy	41.1	6	1.17
Sunbelt Nursery *(Gardening Retailer)*	AMEX	SBN	4 3/4	7 1/8	4	Buy	138.2	NM	(0.80)
Tranzonic Cos. *(Consumer Products)*	AMEX	TNZA	13 7/8	21	13 7/8	Buy	123.1	12	1.19
Tuesday Morning *(Discount Retailer)*	OTC	TUES	10 1/2	17 3/4	8	Buy	174.5	16	0.70
U.S. Banknote *(Printer)*	NYSE	UBK	7 1/4	7 7/8	3 5/8	Buy	172.1	NM	0.43

82

Table 4.5   Growth Stocks to Buy (Continued)

12-Mo. EPS Change	5-Year EPS Growth	Total Assets (mil.)	Book Value Per Share	L-T Debt (mil.)	Shares (mil.)	Beta	Annual Divid	Current Yield	P-E Ratio	Insider (A) & Institutional (B) Ownership		Latest Report Vol./Page
12.1%	-2%	$84.4	$ 9.04	$22.0	4.84	1.79	$0.10	0.6%	17.5	43%	30%	11/102
-65.7	11	76.3	10.28	3.4	4.94	0.34	0.28	2.0	40.7	22	33	11/198
284.6	-41	5.2	0.29	0.0	2.38	0.43	–	–	19.0	33	1	11/221
36.0	26	38.1	5.53	3.7	4.66	1.11	0.60	1.9	19.7	16	54	11/118
84.0	-3	42.1	8.52	1.2	4.60	1.64	–	–	17.3	3	46	11/ 70
-20.0	50	32.0	3.39	2.7	5.85	NM	0.10	1.8	17.2	12	9	11/150
0.0	9	272.7	13.47	67.3	7.95	1.55	–	–	14.1	32	17	11/166
-4.3	19	29.4	6.44	0.0	4.24	1.22	0.40	2.5	14.1	43	20	11/ 71
-54.5	-25	55.4	10.48	2.3	4.26	1.08	–	–	55.0	19	68	11/167
-52.7	30	41.9	9.72	0.6	3.92	1.97	–	–	22.6	11	48	11/119
16.4	16	49.9	8.00	0.0	4.23	NM	–	–	19.6	37	23	11/103
NM	NM	372.0	16.62	181.8	8.74	1.01	0.20	1.8	15.0	15	36	11/ 86
-43.5	2	66.2	7.80	1.8	7.25	1.19	–	–	19.3	15	54	11/135
-8.3	16	50.8	9.92	0.7	3.94	1.00	0.24	1.5	14.5	61	7	11/134
-58.0	66	244.0	5.96	98.5	17.15	1.24	–	–	32.8	27	40	11/151
22.9	10	161.6	4.50	45.0	18.68	0.53	0.12	0.9	22.0	6	21	11/105
-20.8	NM	23.5	4.63	1.0	3.61	NM	0.20	1.1	19.5	2	58	11/152
146.4	-28	81.8	9.15	3.1	7.07	0.89	0.48	2.9	24.3	17	44	11/136
25.4	17	86.0	4.03	16.4	10.37	1.62	0.16	0.8	23.8	27	18	11/106
25.7	NM	139.1	8.13	33.8	5.27	NM	–	–	9.6	4	34	11/ 87
7.3	10	130.8	6.18	35.1	8.29	0.90	0.24	2.2	12.4	43	12	11/137
18.6	16	55.9	6.01	1.7	5.78	1.34	–	–	15.8	24	38	11/153
-15.0	23	15.8	4.47	0.2	2.98	0.86	–	–	10.3	28	29	11/154
49.3	-8	63.3	7.77	16.5	4.30	0.87	0.20	1.3	14.3	51	41	11/120
5.9	44	46.9	3.43	12.2	6.72	0.81	–	–	13.0	23	33	11/ 72
NM	-33	83.5	5.66	19.6	7.45	1.07	0.32	2.5	32.5	32	37	11/210
15.0	92	46.3	5.12	1.5	7.33	NM	–	–	12.6	5	78	11/168
-40.1	NM	103.3	7.16	2.5	5.68	NM	–	–	8.2	41	14	11/ 88
13.6	2	112.4	8.66	9.5	10.40	1.73	–	–	27.2	31	52	11/169
-39.9	-5	255.3	15.25	45.2	7.92	1.05	–	–	23.1	47	46	11/170
17.7	36	49.3	8.25	0.2	5.26	0.77	–	–	21.1	39	33	11/121
1.8	42	71.4	9.51	0.7	4.67	1.38	–	–	12.2	15	66	11/199
58.0	17	81.4	8.28	28.2	3.43	1.41	–	–	11.1	58	18	11/222
-18.8	18	81.3	10.97	6.3	5.83	1.09	0.14	1.2	12.9	16	50	11/183
-13.5	1	35.7	8.93	1.9	3.13	1.04	0.25	2.2	18.0	5	32	11/211
44.7	4	95.0	8.66	20.0	6.99	1.02	0.28	1.1	18.2	35	43	11/138
22.7	32	60.3	5.57	15.9	6.07	1.86	–	–	21.3	35	32	11/184
NM	NM	27.0	3.92	0.1	2.20	NM	–	–	15.2	51	23	11/ 89
-1.1	-4	174.2	19.26	48.4	5.81	0.60	0.50	1.9	13.8	37	47	11/223
34.9	28	43.5	3.89	4.3	8.07	1.21	–	–	22.9	31	18	11/201
31.7	8	45.4	6.28	8.3	4.76	1.35	–	–	25.9	38	29	11/212
60.9	-15	126.3	9.28	36.0	9.08	1.11	0.30	1.6	18.2	58	13	11/185
-10.1	44	45.8	4.70	3.9	3.40	0.94	0.12	1.0	9.9	20	12	11/186
18.2	35	15.5	5.33	0.7	1.64	1.06	–	–	13.9	43	51	11/224
NM	NM	77.3	4.60	1.7	8.48	NM	–	–	NE	10	16	11/122
-3.3	1	63.9	13.20	4.0	3.51	0.89	0.18	1.3	11.7	34	23	11/ 90
-21.3	9	97.2	7.47	11.0	8.64	0.95	–	–	15.0	39	39	11/ 74
NM	NM	231.2	3.62	134.8	17.96	NM	–	–	16.9	14	37	11/213

Figures in bold denote changes since last issue.   NE: Negative earnings. NM: Not meaningful.

A more venturesome investor might weight his or her portfolio with a bigger percentage in growth stocks—perhaps 16.5 percent in growth stocks, 23 percent in growth and income stocks, 35.5 percent in international stocks, 10.5 percent in precious metals, and 14.5 percent in a money fund. This mix would give you an expected return of 14.9 percent with a margin of error of 14.7.

Allocating with individual securities requires a fair commitment to studying the intricacies of the stock market. You must ferret out good blue-chip stocks, sort through the international stock markets, and buy gold-mining stocks or gold bullion to maintain well-blended investments.

IT PAYS TO KEEP YOUR BALANCE

Where should growth investors put their money these days? With most domestic stock market indices hovering around their all-time highs and the "typical" blue-chip stock selling at more than 20 times earnings, the U.S. stock market doesn't look too appealing. Small-caps have soared during the last couple of years and would surely their prices would get beaten down during a stock market sell-off. With Japan being rocked by one political scandal after another and most European economies in the depths of recession, international equities haven't performed very well in recent years. In short, equity investments of any type don't have special appeal these days. Actually, if you ponder long enough, you will probably find good reason to avoid equities no matter what's going on in the financial markets.

BEST APPROACH

Frequently, investors are so nervous about equities that they tend to be underinvested in them at all times. However, history indicates that the best approach to equity investing is to spread capital across all three categories of equities and periodically rebalance that port-folio. That's because the relationship among returns of blue-chip stocks, small-cap stocks and international equities is less than perfect. In other words, when one asset category is performing poorly, another category tends to be performing much better. As a result, equity investors who diversify across categories of equity mutual funds can lower the volatility of return of their portfolio without sacrificing a significant amount of return. As a result, the risk per unit of return of a bal-anced portfolio of equities is reduced to a minimum.

DIVERSIFY YOUR STOCK PORTFOLIO

To illustrate what happens to a balanced portfolio of equities, we tracked the returns of blue-chips, small-caps, and foreign stocks during the last two decades. (See accompanying table.) We then computed the average return and standard deviations of return for each of the three categories and a portfolio consisting of equal dollar investments in each of the three categories (assuming that the portfolio was rebalanced to an equal allocation at the end of each year). Here's what we found.

If you are a conservative investor and wish to mini-mize total risk, the portfolio of choice is U.S. blue-chip stocks. However, this portfolio, as you might expect, also delivered the lowest average annual return (13%). If your goal is to obtain the highest average annual rate of return (17.7% in this case), U.S. small-cap stocks are your cup of tea. Of course, this portfolio is also the riski-est. If your goal is to obtain the greatest return while taking the least amount of risk, the equally balanced portfolio delivers the goods. Note that its average return is 2.4 percentage points greater than that of a blue-chip equity portfolio yet its standard deviation is only 0.8 percentage points greater. As a result, the balanced portfolio's risk per unit of return falls to 1.14.

Although many investors seek to invest where they believe they can earn the greatest short-run returns, prudent investors know that by keeping their balance they can keep their portfolio's return from falling off a cliff because of a forecasting error (i.e., being in the wrong place at precisely the wrong time). In the case of equity investing, this means allocating capital across blue-chip, small-cap and international equities.

A Balanced Approach to Growth Stock Investing

Year	Blue-Chip Stocks	Small-Cap Stocks	International Stocks	Equal Allocation
1972	19.0%	4.4%	40.9%	21.4%
1973	−14.7	−30.9	−14.1	−19.9
1974	−26.5	−19.9	−24.0	−23.5
1975	37.2	52.8	37.5	42.5
1976	23.8	57.4	6.0	29.1
1977	−7.2	25.4	15.6	11.3
1978	6.6	23.5	34.3	21.5
1979	18.4	43.5	12.9	24.9
1980	32.4	39.9	25.1	32.5
1981	−4.9	13.9	−2.1	2.3
1983	21.4	28.8	−0.6	16.3
1982	22.5	39.7	25.1	29.1
1984	6.3	−6.7	5.1	1.6
1985	32.2	24.7	47.2	34.7
1986	18.5	6.9	55.5	26.9
1987	5.2	−9.3	5.0	0.3
1988	16.8	22.9	17.3	19.0
1989	31.5	10.0	23.9	21.8
1990	−3.2	−21.6	−12.0	−12.3
1991	30.5	44.6	11.1	28.7
1992	7.7	23.3	−14.0	15.6
Average Return	13.0%	17.7%	14.1%	15.4%
Standard Deviation	16.7	24.4	21.0	17.5
Risk/ Return	1.29	1.38	1.49	1.14

BLUE-CHIP STOCK VALUES

When you invest in mature companies, you buy a cash cow. These firms have billions in sales and strong cash flows, with current assets of cash and equivalents that far outweigh their current liabilities. They also should be carrying lower levels of debt in relation to their equity or stock value than less mature firms carry. The good firms show an increasing level of sales and earnings per share from year to year, strong profit margins compared to their peers, and high returns on equity. (Return on equity represents the return based on net income in relation to the value of the stockholders' ownership.)

When buying bluer-chip stocks, compare your company's financial statistics with those of its peers, using brokerage-firm reports or those issued by Value Line Investment Survey. Seek out the firms with the best overall numbers, including price-to-earnings multiples that are lower than their peers. You also want to examine new-product developments, increasing marketing budgets, research and development expenditures and promising mergers or acquisitions. Start by accumulating brokerage-firm reports to see what the analysts are recommending and why.

Table 4.6 lists several blue-chip recommended stocks. The companies have long-term growth potential. Some, like Philip Morris, are attractive because they pay above average dividend yields and should show strong earnings growth rates. Other blue-chips like Anheuser-Busch are attractive because stocks are selling a low price to earnings ratios and are expected to grow earnings at a double digit clip.

DIVIDENDS ARE IMPORTANT, TOO

Dividends tell the truth about a company, especially if it is a financially strong firm. You receive cash in the hand

Table 4.6   Good Blue-Chip Stocks

Company	Industry	Exchange	Ticker Symbol	Recent Price
Above Average Yield				
American Home Products	Drugs, Housewares	N	AHP	$63^{1}/_{8}$
Atlanta Gas Light	Natural Gas Utility	N	ATG	$39^{1}/_{4}$
Atlantic Richfield	Integrated Oil	N	ARC	115
Bell South	Telephone Utility	N	BLS	$55^{1}/_{4}$
Bristol-Meyers-Squibb	Pharmaceuticals	N	BMY	$56^{1}/_{2}$
CIGNA	Insurance	N	CI	$60^{1}/_{2}$
Exxon	Integrated Oil	N	XON	$64^{1}/_{8}$
Philip Morris	Tobacco, Food	N	MO	$50^{1}/_{8}$
Texaco	Integrated Oil	N	TX	$63^{1}/_{4}$
Low Price-Earning Ratio				
Anheuser-Busch	Beverages	N	BUD	$46^{3}/_{4}$
Clorox	Household Products	N	CLX	$50^{1}/_{2}$
Deluxe Corp.	Check Printing	N	DLX	$36^{3}/_{4}$
Heinz (H.J.)	Food Processor	N	HNZ	$37^{1}/_{2}$
Kimberly-Clark	Paper Products	N	KMB	$45^{1}/_{2}$
Lilly (Eli)	Pharmaceuticals	N	LLY	45
Merck	Pharmaceuticals	N	MRK	$32^{1}/_{2}$
Sara Lee	Food Processor	N	SLE	25
Schering Plough	Pharmaceuticals	N	SGP	61
High Growth Stocks				
Alberto Culver	Health & Beauty Aids	N	ACV	21
Circus Circus	Gaming, Hotels	N	CIR	39
Countrywide Credit	Financial Services	N	CCR	$31^{1}/_{4}$
Flight Safety	Flight Training	N	FSI	$36^{3}/_{4}$
Home Depot	Building Supplies	N	HD	$44^{1}/_{2}$
International Game Technology	Gaming Devices	N	IGT	35
PepsiCo	Soft Drinks	N	PEP	$37^{5}/_{8}$
Rubbermaid	Household Products	N	RBD	$30^{3}/_{8}$
Tootsie Roll	Candy	N	TR	70
Wrigley (Wm)	Chewing Gum	N	WWY	$38^{1}/_{4}$

Table 4.6   Good Blue-Chip Stocks (Continued)

P/E Ratio	Div'd Yield	5-year Revenue Growth	5-year EPS Growth	Average ROE
13.7	4.5%	7.0%	10.0%	36.5%
17.7	5.3	Nil	3.0	11.0
15.1	4.8	3.0	7.5	20.1
17.3	5.0	4.5	1.5	12.2
18.1	5.1	4.0	11.5	33.6
15.8	5.0	5.0	Nil	7.0
16.2	4.5	9.0	3.0	15.1
9.4	5.2	20.0	23.5	32.8
14.7	5.1	Nil	9.0	13.1
13.4	3.1	7.5%	13.5%	21.5%
16.5	3.6	8.0	8.0	17.6
18.1	3.9	11.5	9.5	24.4
18.4	3.2	9.0	12.0	24.2
18.0	3.6	10.5	14.5	20.2
17.4	5.0	9.5	17.5	33.2
18.4	3.4	16.5	26.5	45.8
17.6	2.2	6.5	16.0	17.6
17.1	2.9	11.0	22.0	35.5
15.2	1.2	14.0%	20.0%	13.5%
27.2	—	22.5	25.0	28.7
12.0	1.3	12.5	16.5	14.5
16.4	1.0	19.0	16.5	16.8
51.0	0.3	29.5	45.0	17.8
40.5	0.2	32.0	34.0	23.4
22.1	1.7	15.5	19.5	23.1
23.8	1.3	13.0	16.0	18.6
22.0	0.5	14.5	16.5	17.5
28.3	1.0	12.5	20.5	28.7

when you collect dividends. You are sharing in the profits of the company and you have the money in the bank. And when you combine dividends with a stock that may grow over the long term, you can boost your total return. You may receive, for example, 5 percent in dividends plus another 10 percent in stock-price appreciation, which translates into a 15-percent total return for the year in this hypothetical example.

Dividends are important investment considerations when selecting stocks for several reasons. First, the majority of exchange-listed companies pay some cash dividends (see Table 4.7). Second, over the last 38 years, for example, 40 percent of a stock's return came from dividends. The total return on the S&P 500 averaged 11.4 percent, which consisted of 4.6 percent dividend yield and 6.8 percent in capital appreciation.

REINVESTING DIVIDENDS BOOSTS RETURNS

Over the long term, when you collect and reinvest these dividends the money compounds and boosts your wealth over the long term. If you invested $1,000 in the S&P 500 index at the beginning of 1926, for example, the investment would be worth $19,366 today if you withdrew the cash from dividends every year. If the dividends were reinvested in new shares, however, your $1,000 investment would have grown to a whopping $347,965.

Table 4.7 Dividend-Paying Nationally Traded Companies

Location	Total Companies	Dividend Payers	Percent
New York Stock Exchange	1,574	1,227	78%
American Stock Exchange	811	338	41.2%
National O-T-C	5,201	2,581	49.6%

Dividends also are an important criteria to consider when evaluating a company. Dividends are real. They are payments that are made in cash. Earnings, however, are subject to accounting whims, even though they are subject to generally accepted accounting principles. Such practices as valuing inventory based on First In First Out (FIFO) or Last In Last Out (LILO), depreciation of assets at different rates and other cost and revenue recognition practices give management a great deal of latitude in reporting earnings. This, however, is not true of dividends. Management always must provide the cash to make dividend payments to stockholders. They just cannot hide behind account magic.

DIVIDENDS ARE MORE STABLE

Dividends also tend to be more stable than a company's reported earnings. The question asked in the boardroom by directors before they pay a dividend is, "Will we be able to maintain the payout come hell or high water?"

The same reasoning is used to determine when and by how much to increase dividend payouts. Most firms only will increase their dividends when they are absolutely certain that the higher payout can be maintained even if earnings take an unexpected tumble.

The stability and predictability of cash dividends are sound reference points that you can use to evaluate stocks and also are an important criteria to consider when valuing the entire stock market. If dividend payouts are increasing on average for the entire market, this is a sign of continued business profitability.

CASH COWS

Table 4.8 provides a list of tried-and-true companies that have been paying cash dividends every year for more than 100 years! Two of these firms have not missed a dividend payment for more than 200 years. What cash machines!

Table 4.8 Tried-and-True Companies

Company	Exchange	Ticker Symbol	Consistent Dividends
Affiliated Publications	NYSE	AFP	1882
Allied Signal	NYSE	ALD	1887
American Property & Casualty	OTC	ALPC	1853
American Express	NYSE	AXP	1870
American T&T	NYSE	T	1881
Amoco	NYSE	AM	1894
Aquarion	NYSE	WTR	1890
Bank of Boston	NYSE	BKB	1784
Bank of New York	NYSE	BK	1785
Bay State Gas	NYSE	BGC	1853
BCE Inc	NYSE	BCE	1881
Boatman's Bancshares	OTC	BOAT	1873
Boston Edison	NYSE	BSE	1890
Carter-Wallace	NYSE	CAR	1883
Chase Manhattan Bank	NYSE	CMB	1848
Cincinnati Bell	NYSE	CSN	1879
Cincinnati Gas & Electric	NYSE	CIN	1853
Coca Cola	NYSE	KO	1893
Connecticut Energy	NYSE	CNE	1850
Connecticut Natural Gas	NYSE	CTG	1851
Consolidated Edison	NYSE	ED	1885
Continental Corp	NYSE	CIC	1854
Core States Financial	OTC	CSFN	1844
Corning Inc	NYSE	GLW	1881
Crestar Financial	OTC	CRFC	1870
Dominion Bankshares	OTC	DMBX	1882
Equitable of Iowa	OTC	EQIC	1889
E'Town Corp	NYSE	ETW	1881
Exxon Corp	NYSE	XON	1882
First of America Bank	NYSE	FOA	1864
First Fidelity Bancorp	NYSE	FFB	1812
Fleet Financial Group	NYSE	FLT	1791
Hartford Steam Boiler Inc	NYSE	HSB	1871
KeyCorp	NYSE	KEY	1841
Lilly (Eli)	NYSE	LLY	1885
Meridian Bancorp	OTC	MRDN	1828
Morgan (J.P.)	NYSE	JPM	1892
Procter & Gamble	NYSE	PG	1891
Providence Energy	NYSE	PUY	1849
Southern N England Telecom	NYSE	SNG	1891
Stanley Works	NYSE	SWK	1877
Star Banc Corp	OTC	STRZ	1863
Times Mirror	NYSE	TMC	1892
Travelers Corp	NYSE	TIC	1864
UGI Corp	NYSE	UGI	1885
U.S. Trust	OTC	USTC	1854
United Water Resources	NYSE	UWR	1886
Washington Gas Light	NYSE	WGL	1852
Westvaco	NYSE	W	1892

GOLD-MINING STOCKS AND BULLION

Canny investors can play the precious-metals market in several ways. Probably the most desirable methods to consider are buying individual gold: mining stocks and buying and storing bullion or American Eagle gold coins. The precious-metals market contains numerous other gold-coin issues, but only Eagles were permissible in an IRA, according to our nation's tax code, so Eagles generally are the best choice.

GOLD STOCKS

Investors concerned with the effects of inflation might want to invest in several well-established mining stocks. Mining stocks have grown at an annual rate of approximately 16 percent over the past ten years, compared to an increase of just 6 percent for gold bullion. Gold-mining stocks have done well for several reasons. Well-operated, rich gold mines enjoy substantial operating leverage, which means the cost of pulling ore out of the ground in a long-life mine (one with 10 to 15 years' worth of ore) has been much lower than the price of gold on the spot market—some firms mine for just $150 to $200 per ounce. As a result, small changes in the price of gold can boost profits dramatically.

Suppose it costs $10 million to operate a mine that annually produces 30,000 ounces of gold. At $400 per ounce, revenues stand at $12 million and pretax earnings are at $2 million. Now suppose the price of gold rises by ten percent to $440 an ounce. The firm's revenues increase to $13.2 million and pretax earnings rise to $3.2 million. As a result, a 10-percent increase in the price of gold has resulted in a startling 60-percent increase in earnings.

Unfortunately, the performance of gold stocks does not always track the price of the metal. Mining stocks are influenced by the overall trend of the equities market, earnings expectations and factors that affect a specific company, such as management, the life of the mine and the efficiency of mining operations, and the risks associated with investments in other countries. As a result, mining stocks are more volatile than bullion. Investors in mining stocks, however, do share in the profits of a company in the form of dividend income and stock-price appreciation. In contrast, gold-bullion investments move more strictly in tandem with inflationary expectations or political or economic crises.

Gold shares are not a proxy for bullion. They are stock and should be considered part of an equity portfolio, while bullion occupies a different portfolio position. When you combine the positions you arrive at diversification. In statistical terms, only a .65 correlation exists between gold-bullion and precious-metals mutual funds. Going into 1993 gold bullion had an expected rate of about 6 percent with a standard deviation of 14 percent, compared to an expected rate of return of 11 percent and a standard deviation of a whopping 35 percent.

This disparity and volatility can work on behalf of investors who want to diversify their investments. A moderate investor might invest 16.5 percent of his or her funds in gold bullion, 1.5 percent in precious-metals mutual funds, 32 percent in corporate-bond funds, 41.5 percent in S&P 500 stocks and 8.5 percent in small-capitalization stocks. This blend would garner an expected rate of return of 13.8 percent with a standard deviation of 12.1 percent, registering 88 percent of the return on the S&P 500 with 25 percent less volatility.

Though precious metals funds' volatility can prove disadvantageous for investors, over different periods they have enjoyed strong performance. For example during ten years ending in 1988 the funds grew at an annual rate of 16.3 percent, while inflation averaged 6 percent, according to Lipper Analytical Services. But over the last five years you lost almost 9 percent a year

Table 4.9   Funds' Annual Growth Rate

December 31, 1978 to December 31, 1988

Funds	Percent annual gain
Gold funds	16.3 percent
Fixed Income	10.7
Balanced	14.5
S&P 500	16.3
Gold Bullion	6.4
CPI	6.0

Source: Lipper Analytical Services, *Barron's Finance and Investment Handbook.*

in your average metals funds. Now in 1993 gold funds were up a whopping 55 percent by the end of April.

You just don't know how gold funds will perform. That makes them a good diversification tool.

SELECTING MINING STOCKS

When selecting mining stocks, professional money managers look for strong financial profiles with low debt-to-equity and high price-to-earnings multiples and strong price-to-cash flow multiples. They also consider the extent of the gold reserves in the company's mines and whether the company is flexible in increasing production.

Over the past ten years, metals have outperformed bullion while inflation was flat because mining companies offset losses by increasing production, for costs of production are much lower than the $350 to $450 price of gold. Also consider what kind of impact a $20 rise in the price of gold would have on corporate earnings. Find out whether your firm sells forward contracts—contracts that agree to sell gold in the future at a specified price. These contracts lock in profits during uncertain periods.

Some of the most profitable mining stocks held by institutional investors include long-lived South African issues and shares of large, well-established North American gold producers such as Battle Mountain and Placer Dome. These companies represent less volatile buys than do producers with shorter mine lives, higher debt-to-equity ratios and more costly production (this category would include American Barrick, Echo Bay, Newmont, and Australian companies).

INVESTING IN THE METAL

If you do invest directly in gold, resolve not to fret over your purchase. Gold bullion prices could languish just as they are for a long time. If inflation should become a serious problem, however, count on gold prices to soar. Temper your burgeoning skepticism with thoughts of 1979, when inflation hit double-digit levels and gold flew from $300 to $800 an ounce almost overnight. Investors who had lost money in bonds when interest rates rose or who had lost money in stocks were protected if they had some gold stashed away.

Historically, gold has proved to be a useful addition to an investment portfolio. According to statistics published by the World Gold Council in New York, a dollar in 1987 would buy only half as much as it had bought 12 years previously, while gold would buy almost twice as much.

Good reason to consider gold a part of any sophisticated investor's portfolio. The metal has a negative attribute, though: It is also an extremely volatile investment, far more so than stocks and bonds. On the plus side, however, gold is a scarce commodity. Some statistics indicate that all the gold ever mined could fit into a cube measuring 56 feet on each side. Gold supplies are growing by less than two percent a year. (In recent years, the total gold supply has averaged about 1,650 metric tons.) A steady market of jewelry manufacturers, industrial and medical users, governments and investors are competing for the limited supply.

HOW TO BUY GOLD

It is as easy to buy gold as it is to open up a bank account: You can purchase gold through any stockbroker or reputable gold dealer. In addition, several investment options and gold-storage programs are available. Bullion bars and wafers range in size from one gram to 400 ounces. Bullion coins, such as the American Eagle, Canadian Maple Leaf, Australian Nugget and Britannia, are available in sizes from one-tenth of an ounce to a full ounce.

OVERSEAS STOCKS

Investing in foreign stocks is best left to the investment pros and money managers who run mutual funds. Foreign stock markets are fraught with risks that make it difficult for the average investor to unearth the best issues. First, you face foreign currency problems. Because stocks are purchased in foreign denominations, if the dollar rises against the other currency, the market value of the investment will drop. Foreign accounting standards and securities laws are far less stringent than those in the United States, leaving investors potentially vulnerable (insider trading, for instance, is generally not frowned on in other countries). You can count on little technical and economic data on your investment, at least by U.S. standards, which can make enlightened decision making difficult. You also have to contend with political or sovereign dangers, such as the danger that a country could freeze assets and prevent you from getting your money.

Fortunately, one easy way to play the foreign stock market exists: You can buy shares in closed-end foreign stock funds.

CLOSED-END OVERSEAS STOCK FUNDS

Closed-end mutual funds essentially are publicly traded investment companies. Firms sell a fixed number of shares in these funds, shares that are traded on our major stock exchanges. The funds invest in a portfolio of stocks, with their share price based on the net asset value of that portfolio. When you invest in a closed-end fund, a discrepancy between the closed-end fund price and its net asset value may occur, because brokers do not push the sale of these funds too aggressively. Studies have shown that when you buy a closed-end fund that is trading below its historical average discount to net-asset value, you will profit when the discount narrows. When you buy at a discount to net-asset value, you essentially are buying something for less than it is worth—85 cents to 90 cents on the dollar or even less. Therefore, by all means, keep your eye on these funds.

Several closed-end foreign-country funds are traded on the U.S. stock exchanges. You can find information on these funds from your stockbroker, the S&P reports and the Value Line Investment Survey available at your local library.

By investing in a basket of these closed-end funds, you can create a diversified portfolio of foreign securities to add to your asset-allocation mix. The Asia Pacific Fund and Scudder New Asia Fund, for example, invest in a diversified portfolio of Asian stocks. You also can invest in the France Fund, the Germany Fund, the Helvetica Fund (which invests in the Swiss stock market), the Italy Fund, the Korea Fund, the Scandinavian Fund, and the Taiwan Fund.

ADRs

You also can invest in individual foreign companies that have their stock traded on our major exchanges in the form of American Depository Receipts (ADRs).

An ADR is a negotiable certificate that represents an ownership of shares in a non-U.S. company. ADRs trade in U.S. dollars on the U.S. securities markets; they are the investors' alternative to directly purchasing shares in foreign corporations traded on the overseas stock markets. ADRs basically function as a receipt for shares in these companies, and they entitle a shareholder to all pursuant dividends and capital gains. You can invest in some well-known foreign firms this way, including Germany's Deutsche Bank and Volkswagen; Japanese firms such as Daiwa, Fuji Film, Hitachi, Nissan Motor Co., or Sharp Corporation; British firms such as Bass Limited and B.A.T. Industries; Italy's automaker Fiat; or the Netherlands' European chemical giant, Akzo.

BOND BASICS

When you buy a bond, you lend a company money and become one of the issuing firm's creditors. When you borrow money from a bank, you pay interest for the privilege of using the bank's money. Corporations, the U.S. government and state and local governments must do the same thing: They raise money by issuing bonds. A bond is an IOU. The issuer pays the holder semiannual interest on the loan at a specified rate for a specified period of time. Issuers borrow money over the long term—15 to 30 years or thereabouts—by issuing debt securities. Issuers also borrow for the short term—five to ten years—by selling notes. You can buy a bond or note for as little as $1,000. The issuing corporation may use the money to finance an expansion, purchase new equipment, or increase production.

UNDERSTANDING BOND YIELDS

Bonds have two yields: the current yield and the yield to maturity. The current yield is the rate of interest income you receive on a $1,000 investment. You buy a bond with a current yield of nine percent, for example, and you buy the bond at par value. Par value is the initial offering price of the bond before the bond's price changes because of fluctuations in prevailing interest rates. A bond that pays $90 in interest (this rate is known as the coupon rate), for instance, on a $1,000 bond currently yields nine percent. If you bought the bond in the secondary market and it was priced at $980, the current yield would be $90 divided by $980, which equals a current yield of 9.18 percent.

You also have to consider a bond's yield to maturity. Bonds pay semiannual interest over a specific time period. As a result, you must factor in the compounding of interest. At par, the current yield and yield to maturity of a bond are the same. After the price of the bond changes, however, the yield to maturity will reflect not only the semiannual compounding of interest, but also the capital gain or loss on the security itself. When a bond is purchased at a discount or below par value, the yield to maturity will be greater than the current yield. This discrepancy occurs because the buyer is collecting interest payments and, when the bond matures, will collect par value, representing a capital gain over the purchase price. If you buy a bond that sells for more than par, the yield to maturity will be less than the current yield, because you paid more than par value for the bond but just collect par value at maturity.

If you bought a bond with a nine-percent current yield at $980, with 19 years to maturity remaining, the yield to maturity would be 9.23 percent. If you bought the same bond for $1,020, the yield to maturity would equal 8.78 percent.

FIXED-INCOME RISK

Investors face two major types of risks when they invest in bonds: interest-rate risk and credit risk. Interest rates and bond prices move in opposite directions—when rates rise, bond prices drop. Conversely, when rates decline, bond prices rise. The longer the maturity of the bond, the bigger the price decline or rise when interest rates change.

Credit risk is the ability of the bond issuer to keep up payments, both of principal and interest. A danger buyers of long-term bonds face is that the issuer could go bankrupt before the bond matures. Bondholders thus can theoretically lose their entire investment, both principal and interest. Bondholders are first in line as creditors of a company, however, and bond covenants state that their lenders take priority in collecting money from the sale of assets to cover debts.

REDUCING INTEREST-RATE RISK

Investors can reduce interest-rate risk by investing in short-term maturities, which contain less price volatility. If you owned a bond that paid today's current rates and matured in 30 years and interest rates rose 1 percent, the market value of your bond would decline 9.4 percent in value. By contrast a bond with that matures in just five years would lose 3.8 percent in value.

You may ask how a note and a bond both can pay nine percent. The answer is that sometimes the market professionals value short-term debt securities more than long-term bonds because they think interest rates will be rising. As a result, tight money policy may drive up short-term rates. When this happens, short-term maturities can out-yield long-term bonds. That's what happened during the first half of 1989. Today, however the yield curve is flattening out. Eventually we might see an inverted yield curve again, if short-term rates rise or if long-term rates fall.

REDUCING CREDIT RISK

You also can take steps to reduce credit risk and assess the financial strength of a bond issuer. One quick rule of thumb is that the higher the bond yield, the greater the risk. If you keep that axiom in mind when purchasing bonds, you will greatly reduce your chances of being caught in a bond default. Financially weak companies must compensate investors who risk loaning them money by paying higher rates. You, the buyer, are gambling that, over the long term, the company will be able to keep up the payments. You should be wary of any issuer that pays more than four percent interest above comparable Treasury securities.

Fortunately, Standard & Poor's and Moody's, two bond-credit analysis firms, rate bonds. You can obtain these bond rates from your broker; ratings also are listed in the bond's prospectus. These agencies evaluate a firm's financial strength to see whether it has the cash flow and income to make timely payments of both principal and interest. The top-rated bonds also obtain bank letters of credit to back them, in which banks promise to step in and pay off the debt in the event of problems. In practice, of course, a bank is not going to back a company's debt obligations unless it is one of the most financially sound companies in the business.

You can use the S&P and Moody's rates to assess the creditworthiness of a bond issuer. The following table lists how bonds are rated.

Table 4.10   Bond Ratings

Moody's	S&P	Creditworthiness
Aaa	AAA	Highest grade
Aa	AA	High grade
A	A	Medium grade
Baa	BBB	Minimum investment grade
Ba	BB	Speculative grade
B	B	Highly speculative
Caa	CCC	Poor quality
Ca	CC	Bonds in default

What type of bonds should you pick when allocating assets? The answer is obvious. The lowest-risk, best corporate bonds to buy are AAA- and Aaa-rated issues. You might earn a little less yield, but the investments are safer and more liquid. If you need cash, triple-a rated bonds easily can be sold. These issuers are large, blue-chip multinational corporations, which offer minimal risk of default.

TREASURY BONDS AVOID CREDIT RISK

U.S. Treasury securities are backed "full faith and credit" against default by everyone's most enduring relative, Uncle Sam. Treasury bond prices do change with the level of interest rates, so you still are exposed to interest-rate risk. You can, however, mitigate this risk by investing in T-bills, which mature in three months to a year, or T-bonds, which offer maturities of up to ten years.

Treasury bills are short-term government securities bearing maturities ranging from 91 days to one year. They are sold at a discount in denominations of $10,000. The discount simply means that you invest in these bills at lower than face value and collect accumulated interest at maturity. If you bought a one-year T-bill at 3.5 percent, you would pay $9,650 for your bill and collect $10,000 one year later. Three hundred and fifty dollars is 3.5 percent of $10,000.

Treasury notes bear longer maturities than T-bills. They mature in two to ten years and pay semiannual interest. T-notes can be bought for $1,000 for maturities longer than four years; two- and three-year T-notes will cost $5,000 to buy.

Treasury-bond maturities are longer than ten years. They pay semiannual interest and the minimum investment is only $1,000. T-bonds generally pay higher rates than bills and notes do, except under certain abnormal conditions dictated by the monetary policies of the

Federal Reserve Bank. T-bond prices are more volatile than those of other Treasury securities.

If you do not want to worry about any credit risk, buy Treasury securities when you allocate the fixed-income portion of your assets. The correlations between Treasury bonds and corporate bonds are very high: The two investments behave almost identically. Treasury securities reduce credit risk and also are exempt from state and local income taxes.

A WORD ABOUT INFLATION AND STOCK PRICES: PUBLIC ENEMY NUMBER ONE

Here's a short investment quiz. Score 100 points and stand at the head of the class if you answer correctly. Give yourself a big fat zero and put on the dunce cap if you respond incorrectly.

What's an investor's biggest enemy?

(1) Negative earnings surprises
(2) Economic recessions
(3) Democratic Presidents
(4) Stockbrokers
(5) Themselves
(6) None of the above

Sorry for the trick question. The correct answer is none of the above. The number one enemy of all investors (and savers and consumers as well) is inflation. Spiraling price increases at the producer and consumer level confound the economic delivery system, create difficulties in making economic forecasts, erode investment returns, and erode the standard of living of nearly everyone. While real assets tend to appreciate during periods of hyper-inflation, rarely do incomes keep pace with increases in the CPI. As a result, even real asset holders tend to lose during a period marked by abnormally high rates of inflation, even though they lose less than everyone else.

Interestingly, no one can agree upon the definition of inflation these days. Technically speaking, of course, inflation is defined as any increase in consumer and producer prices. Thus, what people mean by "inflation" is "intolerable inflation." Very few people would be concerned if consumer prices were growing by 1 or 2 percent per year. However, what if they grow at a 3 percent annual rate? What about 5 percent? In other words, how much inflation can an economic system stand?

WE HAVE TO LIVE WITH SOME INFLATION

Back in the 1950s, the Commission on Money and Credit defined the acceptable threshold of CPI increases at about 1.5 percent. In the 1970s, 5 percent marked the threshold of concern. Today, that level seems to be about 3 percent as announced increases at higher annual rates cause quite a stir in financial circles.

As a point of reference, the CPI has grown at a 3.1 percent compound annual rate since the late 1920s. Its greatest annual rate of increase (18.2 percent) occurred in 1946. Its lowest rate, a 10.3 percent *decline,* occurred in 1932. The worst 10-year period of inflation spanned 1973 through 1982, during which the CPI rose by 8.7 percent annually, a total of 130 percent. During the most benign 10-year period (1926–1935), the CPI *declined* at a 2.6 percent annual rate. By the end of that period, consumer prices had tumbled a total of 23 percent. Interestingly, common stock returns tend to be below par during periods marked by either deflation or hyper-inflation. During the 1973–1982 period, the S&P 500 Index returned a below-average 6.7 percent and during the 1926–1935 period, this hypothetical portfolio of blue-chip stocks returned an average of 5.9 percent. So, whenever the rate of increase in the CPI strays too far from its norm, common stock investors tend to suffer.

WHEN BOND FUND INVESTORS WIN

As would be expected, fixed-income investors "win" during periods of deflation and lose during periods of inflation. For example, government bonds returned an average of 5.0 percent between 1926 and 1935. Given that consumer prices were declining by 2.6 percent annually during that period, long-term government bond investors' real return ballooned to 7.6 percent. During the hyper-inflation years (1972–1983), long-term government bonds returned an average of 5.3 percent. Subtracting the 8.7 percent annual rate of increase in the CPI produces an annual real rate of return of *minus* 3.4 percent.

Annual Rates of Inflation: 1930–Present

Period	Compound Annual Rate
1930s	−2.9%
1940s	5.4
1950s	2.2
1960s	2.5
1970s	7.4
1980s	5.1
1990s	4.0
Average	3.1%

WHEN STOCK FUND INVESTORS WIN

Given the rate of inflation today, are stocks a good or bad investment? To answer this question, we turned to investment theory and a reading of investment history. Investment theory tells that, all other things equal, the higher the rate of return on alternative investments (e.g., bonds), the lower will be the stock market's price-earnings ratio. Since inflation is the one variable that drives interest rates higher, one would expect to find an inverse relationship between market price-earnings multiples and the rate of inflation. That is exactly what we found to be true during the last sixty years.

Market Price/Earnings Multiples and the Rate of Inflation

Inflation Range	Average p/e Multiple
0.0% to 2.0%	15.8
2.1 to 4.0	14.1
4.1 to 6.0	12.1
6.1 to 8.0	12.2
8.1 to 10.0	10.4
Above 10.0	8.2

Correlational analysis indicates that, on average, the market's price/earnings ratio *declines* by about 0.7 times earnings per share for every 100 basis point increase in the rate of inflation. (One basis point equals 0.01 percent). In general, the relationship between the market's p/e ratio and changes in the consumer price index is as follows:

p/e Ratio = 16.2 − 0.7 (percent change in CPI).

The model indicates that at a zero percent rate of inflation, the Standard & Poor's 500 Index (a proxy for the stock market) should sell at 16.2 times per share earnings. A 4.0 percent rate of change in the CPI is generally associated with a market p/e of 13.4. Furthermore, if the rate of inflation were to increase to a 6.0 percent annual rate, the market p/e multiple would fall to 12 times earnings.

Although most investors know that there is an inverse relationship between valuations in the stock market and the rate of inflation (i.e., the greater the rate of inflation the lower is the market's price-earnings ratio), the exact multiple one should associate with a particular rate of inflation has not been specifically determined. However, our analyses indicate that the market's price-earnings ratio should change by about one point for every 100 basis point change in the rate of inflation.

CHAPTER 5

Mutual Funds

The safest way to double your money, a wit once observed, is to fold it over once and put it in your pocket.

Stock market and bond-market profits undoubtedly are enticing. We have all heard stories around the office or the health club about someone with a hot tip who doubled his or her money in a takeover play or borrowed money from a broker and caught a bond-market rally at the right time.

The sobering fact of the matter is that the average investor is gambling with his or her hard-earned money when he or she takes a chance on a hot investment. Play the state lottery if you want to bet a dollar on making several hundred thousand dollars. If you would like to meet your financial objectives without taking a chance on accidentally cracking your nest egg, however, investing in mutual funds is about the surest way to do it. For the investor who lacks the time or expertise to select individual securities for asset allocation, mutual funds may be the best bet in the equities market.

FUNDS DIVERSIFY FOR YOU

Mutual funds pool investors' money and diversify into many more securities than an individual could hope to buy. This makes funds ideal asset-allocation vehicles for the average investor and saver. The diversification in stock funds reduces nonmarket risk or the risk that if a few stocks do poorly, the overall investment will suffer. Most mutual funds hold more than 50 securities in their portfolios—some hold a couple of hundred split up among different industries. Investors benefit because professional money managers and researchers oversee their investments.

In addition, with mutual funds you can allocate substantial portions of your assets and still keep them all under one roof. Most mutual-funds companies contain a stable of stock, bond, precious metals and overseas securities funds. You can divide up your investment pie within one mutual-funds family.

PAY YOURSELF INSTEAD OF YOUR BROKER

No-load mutual funds are ideal investment vehicles for asset allocation. You pay no up-front sales commission, and for a one-half-percent to one percent management fee, you receive professional management, research, and diversification.

Currently, more than 3,000 mutual funds are on the market, about a third of which are no-load. You buy these funds directly from the firm by calling a tollfree number and placing your order. Load funds can be purchased through stockbrokers and financial planners; you pay an up-front sales charge ranging from three to eight percent. Some funds carry back-end or deferred sales changes that stay in effect for five years or more. If you cash in within that time, you will have to pay. In addition, load funds also carry 12b-1 charges or sales-distribution fees. These run as high as one percent of assets and are deducted annually from the fund. Over a 20-year period, that annual one percent deduction would be equivalent to paying an up-front charge of 20 percent.

With all these charges, it is best to remain with no-load funds or at least low-load funds. If you must pay $850 on a $10,000 investment, your investment is going to be behind from the start. The fund will have to gain 9.3 percent just for you to break even on your initial investment. If you dollar cost average by putting the same amount of money into a load fund each month, you really will have a hard time catching up.

Over the long term, paying a front-end load can result in a tremendous amount of lost income. Those single-digit sales charges can seem innocuous. According to a study conducted by Sheldon Jacobs, publisher of *The Handbook For No-Load Fund Investors,* if both a load and no-load fund grew at ten percent annually for ten years, you would have earned $2,204 more in the no-load fund because the other fund deducted $850 from the initial $10,000 investment before you started earning money.

STALKING THE WILD NO-LOAD FUND

You can spot no-load funds in the business section of the newspaper under the section that lists mutual-funds prices (see Figure 5.2). The first column lists the fund's name. The next lists the fund's net asset value (NAV), which is what the fund was worth at the close of the preceding business day. The NAV is calculated by dividing the market value of the fund's total assets, less liabilities, by the number of outstanding shares.

The offering or share price is what you would pay if the fund charged an up-front commission or load. If XYZ

Figure 5.1 **Comparison of $10,000 investment in two mutual funds each growing ten percent per year, compounded annually**

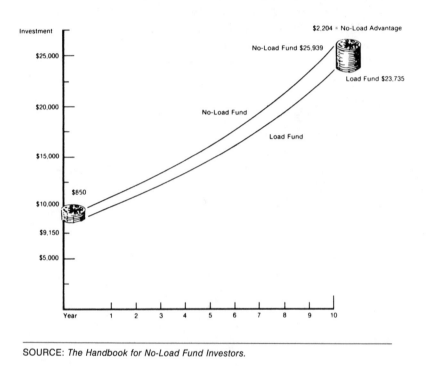

SOURCE: *The Handbook for No-Load Fund Investors.*

---

fund had an NAV of $16.87 and an offering price of $17.43, you would pay a 3.3 percent load to buy into the fund. The ABC fund, however, has no offering price, which means that you pay the NAV sans load. The last column in this section shows the price change in NAV from the previous day—perhaps ABC's NAV changed 14 cents yesterday.

No-load mutual funds make sense. Not only can they save you money, but also the concept of the mutual-funds family makes it easy to allocate assets. Approximately 40

Figure 5.2   **How to Read Newspaper Quotations**

It is very easy to check the performance of your mutual fund by turning to the fund tables in the financial sections of most daily newspapers. A typical listing is illustrated below. The first column shows the fund's abbreviated name. Several funds under a single heading indicate a family of funds.

The second column is the Net Asset Value (NAV). This is what a share of a fund was worth at the close of the preceding day's trading. It is computed by dividing the market value of the fund's total assets, less liabilities, by the number of shares outstanding.

The offer price, sometimes called the buy or asked price, is what you would pay for a share of the fund. If a fund charges a commission or load, the offer price is the NAV plus any sales charge. An NL for no-load appears in this column when there is no initial sales load, and the buy price is the same as the NAV.

The last column is the amount the NAV has risen or fallen compared with the previous trading day. In the example, ABC Fund is worth $13.25, is a no-load fund, and gained 14 cents a share.

Other symbols seen in newspaper listings are usually explained with the tables as shown in the example. During 1988 the National Association of Securities Dealers (NASD), to make the listings more informative, added "p" to the footnote codes to identify funds with 12(b)-1 plans.

Mutual Funds

HOW TO READ MUTUAL FUND TABLES — The following quotations, supplied by the NASD, New York, via the Associated Press, are the prices at which these securities could have been sold (net asset value) or bought (value plus sales charge). "Chg." means the change from the previous day's "sell" quotation. "NL" means "no initial load" or no initial charge., x means ex-dividended, r—redemption charge may apply, f—previous day's quotation, p—distribution costs apply (12b-1 fee), d—ex-distribution, a fund's redemption price, NAV—net asset value per share, z—not available, t—both p and r.

Funds	NAV	Offer Price	NAV Chg.	Funds	NAV	Offer Price	NAV Chg.	Funds	NA
Rkeis				ABC Fund	13.25	NL +	.14	Growal	
Ykdo x	15.39	NL +	.18	XYZ Fund	16.87	17.43 -	.07	Oslap	15.
Nakew	12.39	NL +	.02	Caleme	17.25	NL +	.02	Ramalq	12.
Mswlzet	14.70	NL +	.08	Dsueui	36.50	NL +	.01	Bdwol t	14
Iksem f	27.54	NL +	.11	Bevehak				Dalina	27
Qusoel									
Psusjeae	16.32	17							
Waratsge	23.45	25							
Gsisk r	31.09	34							
Asdzrd	21.67	22							
Vdjsue									
Gauad p	12.23	N							
Ragataq	16.02	N							

Funds	NAV	Offer Price	NAV Chg.
ABC Fund	13.25	NL +	.14
XYZ Fund	16.87	17.43 -	.07

Source: Mutual Fund Education Alliance

---

no-load mutual-funds families are on the market today. These funds groups offer a wide variety of funds to choose from, ranging from money funds to stock, bond and precious-metals funds. With just a telephone call, you can instruct your funds group to switch money from one fund to another or to make redemptions. This switching capability makes it very easy for an investor to make asset-allocation decisions.

OTHER ADVANTAGES

Several other reasons why mutual-funds investing makes sense for the average investor are as follows:

Professional Management. Securities funds represent a professionally managed, diversified portfolio of stocks, bonds or both. Mutual-funds portfolio managers are trained in finance, with years of experience managing portfolios. Many funds provide in-house analysts and research staffs that review financial and economic data and select securities representing the best value for capital appreciation or income. Many mutual-funds companies offer financial incentives to portfolio managers to outperform the general market.

Diversification. A diversified portfolio of stocks or bonds reduces risk. According to financial research, 60 percent of the time a stock's price moves in tandem with the overall market. That is what we called market risk in chapter 1. Another 20 to 30 percent of a security price is determined by specific information about a company and/or its industry. Luck is the remaining factor that can influence a stock's price—that is what we called nonmarket risk in Chapter 1.

Investors should not expect to get rich quick from mutual-funds investments. During the past ten years, an unusual boom in stock and bond prices has occurred as a result of the bull market. According to Lipper Analytical Services, the average equity fund has gained

332 percent with all dividends and capital gains reinvested. Bond funds were up 244 percent.

LONG-TERM PERFORMANCE

Mutual-funds share prices can be volatile. Historically, however, financial research has shown that over the past 60 years, equity assets have experienced the largest net gain of any class of investment. According to Ibboston Associates from 1926 through 1992, the S&P 500 stock index earned an annual rate of 10 percent. Long-term corporate bonds averaged 5 percent, long-term government bonds averaged 4.3 percent, and U.S. T-bills averaged 3.5 percent.

Clearly, an investment in common stocks at any time is probably a smart move. At a 10 percent rate of return, money doubles every 7.2 years. If you invested $3,000 in a typical fund for 25 years, you would amass a retirement kitty of over $314,000 at this rate. That money, if invested in a retirement or pension plan, would grow tax-deferred until distributions are taken at retirement.

WIDE PRICE SWINGS PAY OFF

Although common stocks historically have shown the highest returns among investments, stocks are volatile. According to the Ibbotson study, common stocks can average plus or minus 21 percent in any given year. Investors must beware of placing fresh cash into a losing market.

Bonds exhibited less price volatility, but bond returns also were lower. Total returns on corporate bonds, which include reinvestment of dividends and price appreciation, can range between plus or minus 8.5 percent; government bonds returns are about the same.

Portfolio managers exert little control over market risk or the uncertainty of the financial sectors. If the stock market is moving up, eight or nine times out of ten, their portfolios will register gains. As of August of 1987, the year-to-date return on all equity funds, according to Lipper, was 30 percent, while the S&P 500 gained 36 percent.

Diversification, however, will protect investors against nonmarket risk. If a portfolio manager loaded up on a limited number of issues, a few losers could greatly reduce the return on the portfolio. Most well-diversified mutual funds with assets of more than $200 million will hold anywhere from 50 to several hundred stocks. The larger mutual funds also typically hold a portfolio that will correlate 70 to 80 percent with the S&P 500. By holding a large number of issues and maintaining a portfolio that tracks the broader market, fund managers ensure that a few poorly performing issues will not hurt the performance of the fund.

Liquidity. Mutual funds offer investors liquidity. You can turn your investment back into cash at any time. The majority of investment companies offer a stable of mutual funds with different investment objectives, so investors always can make a telephone call and switch from their present fund into another as their financial needs or investment conditions change. Or they can redeem shares and receive a check with a simple telephone call.

Low Cost. Mutual funds represent a low-cost way to invest in the financial markets. Management fees for running the portfolio usually range from .5 percent to 1 percent, depending on the total assets in the fund. Several hundred no-load mutual funds are on the market in which you pay no other front-end or back-end sales charge.

Systematic Investment or Withdrawal. You regularly can have money from your bank Now account or money fund deposited in a mutual fund. You also can have funds

116

systematically redeemed from your fund—monthly, for example—if you need income when you retire.

TYPES OF MUTUAL FUNDS

With more than 2,000 mutual funds on the market, individual investors can match their risk level and investment goals with the mutual funds' objectives. While no two mutual funds are exactly alike, they fall into several broad-based categories.

Aggressive-Growth Funds. These funds, which are the riskiest equity funds, seek maximum capital appreciation and provide little current income to investors. Typically, aggressive-growth funds invest in new companies or existing growth companies that are traded on the over-the-counter stock market. They also may invest in companies or industries that are out of favor regardless of the capitalization or market value of the stock, because of the profit potential in undervalued or overlooked stocks.

During the 1960s, aggressive-stock funds were called "go-go" funds. Things have not changed. These funds can outperform the market by as much as 25 to 30 percent, especially during the initial stages of a bull market. On the other hand, investors can lose just as much if the portfolio manager's stock selection fares poorly or the overall market is in a steep decline. The Value Line Leveraged Growth Fund, which invest in companies that might become tomorrow's blue-chips, has registered an annual rate of return of 10.6 percent over the past ten years. At the start of the last bull market in 1982, the fund gained 26 percent and earned 7 percent more than the S&P 500. In 1988, though, the fund underperformed the S&P 500. Over the past three years ending in April of 1993, the fund also outpaced the market average, but year-to-date the Leverage Growth fund is underperforming.

Growth Funds. Like their aggressive cousins, growth funds seek capital appreciation. They usually

117

are less risky because the funds invest in more well-seasoned companies that also pay dividends. Income from a growth fund is a secondary consideration, however. The low-load Fidelity Magellan Fund, the top-performing growth fund over the past ten years, currently yields 1.9 percent and holds stock in firms such as IBM, Ford Motor, General Motors, Merck, and Eastman Kodak.

Growth and Income Funds. These funds invest in well-seasoned blue-chip companies with records of paying dividends. This type of fund is less risky than growth-oriented funds are because it invests in companies with larger capitalization that have the cash flow to pay shareholder dividends. In addition, the high dividend yields of three percent or more enable investors to reinvest income in new shares, which can boost up total return. Dividends also can cushion the blow in the event of a market decline.

Balanced Funds. These funds focus on preservation of principal. A balanced fund will invest in a mixed portfolio with fixed percentages in common stock, preferred stock, and bonds. Balanced funds are less volatile than the overall market, fluctuating less than the S&P 500 or the Dow Jones Industrial Average. Investors receive income from high-yielding equities and fixed-income securities. Balanced funds generally will underperform during a bull market but outperform the market during a recession.

Total Return Funds. These funds are a hybrid form of balanced fund that provides investors with greater opportunities for profit. Total-return portfolio managers enjoy greater flexibility than balanced-fund managers. They can move funds between stocks and fixed-income securities in any percentage that they choose as conditions change. In 1981, during a period of tight money, the Strong Total Return Fund aimed for high short-term interest rates by investing almost 100 percent in commercial paper. As interest rates fell, the fund picked up capital gains in bonds and moved into equities. Currently, the fund has 70 percent of its $700 million portfolio in common stocks, 20 percent in intermediate-term bonds and 10 percent in cash.

Income Funds. These funds seek a high level of current income for shareholders by investing in high dividend–paying common stock and government and corporate bonds. Income funds can invest up to 60 percent of their assets in equities and up to 75 percent in bonds. They currently are yielding between three and nine percent. The Franklin Income Fund, for example, is yielding 8 percent and is about 33 percent invested in utility stocks, with the remainder in cash and debt securities. Because income funds hold a large portfolio of income-paying stock, they are less volatile than the stock market as a whole. They also are more sensitive, however, to changes in interest rates.

Bond Funds. Bond funds offer several different variations in both the corporate and tax-exempt sectors. Some invest in long-term bonds, others in intermediate- and short-term notes. Some bond funds invest in only the most creditworthy issuers—companies with debt obligations rated A to triple A by Standard & Poor's and Moody's. Bonds rated BB or lower are called "junk" bonds. Currently, mutual funds that invest in junk bonds are yielding 9 to 10 percent, or 3.5 percent more than Treasury securities.

Other bond funds invest in government securities. Funds that invest solely in U.S. Treasury securities carry no credit or default risk because the bonds are guaranteed by the government. Government securities funds also invest in U.S. government-agency debt obligations—primarily bonds issued by the Federal Home Loan Bank Board (FHLBB), the Government National Mortgage Association (GNMA), the Federal National Mortgage Association (FNMA) and the Federal Home Loan Mortgage Corporation (FHLMC).

Government securities bond funds usually pay about
$1/2$ percent more interest than do Treasury bonds for several reasons. First, U.S. government-agency debt carries
an implied moral obligation, but not a full faith and
credit obligation, that the federal government will back
up any defaults. Second, many government agencies
issue mortgage bonds. As a result, both principal and
interest are paid off to investors during the lifetime of
the bond. Government-mortgage bond funds reinvest
the principal and may distribute the interest to
investors. Because of the danger of repayment of both
principal and interest during times of rising interest
rates, the marketplace demands higher yields.
Currently, for example, GNMA bonds are yielding about
8 percent, compared to 6.7 percent on long-term
Treasury bonds.

Bond funds are not without risk. Although only a low
correlation exists between bond and equity returns,
bond funds can be just as volatile as stocks. Bond prices
move in opposition to interest rates; consequently, when
interest rates rise, bond prices fall. The longer the
maturity of the bond, the greater the price volatility.

If interest rates rose 1 percent, for example, the price of
a bond fund with a 6 percent yield and average maturity
of 20 years would decline 10.15 percent. A fund that had
a five-year maturity would drop 4.25 percent in value.

Money-market Funds. Money funds invest in short-term money-market instruments, such as T-bills, certificates of deposit (CDs), commercial paper and repurchase
agreements that are more than 100 percent collateralized. Because the funds are required to carry an average
maturity of fewer than 125 days, they can maintain an
unchanging net asset value of $1 per share. Money funds
offer no price volatility, but they also pay lower yields
than long-term bonds under most conditions. Money
funds include check-writing privileges and can be used to
concentrate daily cash balances or to pay bills.

Overseas Mutual Funds. These funds appear in two forms. Global funds invest in both the U.S. and the overseas stock markets. International funds exclude U.S. stocks and bonds from their portfolios. These funds offer an extra layer of diversification to mutual-funds holdings. Many of the world's stock markets lead or lag behind the U.S. market, so losses in the United States may be offset by gains on other shores. Overseas mutual funds, however, carry their own additional risks. Changes in the value of the dollar in relation to other currencies can affect the market value of overseas holdings. Investors also face political perils, as well as the difficulty of contending with the peculiar volatility of nonnative markets.

Sector Funds. Sector funds are specialized mutual funds. They invest in specific industrial sectors, such as health care, banking, technology, precious metals, and chemicals and drugs. Fidelity Investments, Vanguard, and Financial Programs are three mutual-funds groups that contain stables of sector funds. Fidelity Investments offers the largest group of these funds, providing investors with 35 sectors to choose from. Investors also are given the option of selling the mutual funds on the short side via Fidelity's discount-brokerage operation, which means that they can borrow shares of a fund and sell them, with the hope of buying them back in the future at a lower price.

Sector funds are a high-risk gambit because they provide no industry diversification. If a specific industry is doing well, investors profit, but if it slumps, investors easily can lose their shirts. A few years ago, when Fidelity Technology racked up double-digit gains, money flowed into the fund at an unprecedented rate. It promptly lost 50 percent of its value. As a result of these risks, experts advise that only sophisticated investors purchase sector funds.

Precious-metals mutual funds, on the other hand, though technically limited to a specific "sector," often are considered a long-term inflation hedge. Financial planners may recommend that investors keep five percent of their assets in precious metals. In times of high inflation, bonds and stocks lose value rapidly, but gold and gold-related assets appreciate.

Other types of sector funds can be used judiciously. During bear markets and recessions, sectors with a stable or inelastic demand for goods may make fine safe harbors. Traditionally, utilities, defense, food, soaps, tobacco, and beverages are considered defensive investment sectors.

THE BEST FUNDS FOR YOUR PORTFOLIO

All mutual funds are not created equal. Once you have decided on what type of fund you want to buy, you cannot just grab up shares of the Bull Moose Growth Stock Fund or the First Aid Bond Fund and be content that you have diversified properly. Here are some important criteria to consider before you invest.

- Is the fund part of a no-load mutual funds family? If it is, you can diversify under one roof. For record-keeping purposes, consolidation will make your life easier.
- Read the prospectus and make sure the fund's investment objectives match yours.
- Look at the fund's record and examine its performance over at least ten years, if possible. Look for consistency in returns and check to see how the fund performed in down markets, such as those of 1974, 1981, 1987, and 1990. Two funds may have the same average rates of return over the years, but one may be up 30 percent one year and down 10 percent in another, while the alternative fund attained the same average with less volatility.

You want a fund that has performed consistently over the years. You also can check the fund's beta value and standard deviation or margin of error. Remember, the higher the beta and margin of error in performance, the greater the risk. The S&P 500 has a beta value of one, so funds with higher betas will have an atypically high upside potential as well as an atypical risk in bear markets. Funds with beta values of less than one will perform better than average in down markets. Ask a fund representative for the information or find it in the *Mutual Fund Sourcebook,* a directory that lists betas, standard deviations, and risk rankings. (Morningstar Mutual Funds, Morningstar, Inc., 53 West Jackson Street, Suite 460, Chicago, Illinois 60604.) Another excellent source to consider is CDA/Wiesenberger (1355 Piccard Dr., Rockville, Maryland 20850.)

The fund's margin of error tells you the range of profit or loss that will occur in the fund about 68 percent of the time. In bond funds, look for a fund that has a low margin of error—it will be less volatile than average. With stock funds, look for the best return coupled with the lowest margin of error, or rate of return per unit of risk. If fund A showed an annual rate of return over the past five years of 12 percent and a margin of error of 3 percent, your return per unit of risk would be 4 percent. If fund B showed a 16 percent annual return with a 10 percent margin of error, your return per unit of risk would be only 1.6.

Which fund would you select—one with more consistent returns because of a lower margin of error or one that might pay off at a high rate one year but swing wildly in the opposite direction the next year? Most prudent investors who want to allocate assets would pick the consistent performer.

- Notice the fund's expense ratio, which will show how much it costs to operate the fund in relation to its assets. The average expense ratio is about one percent, but the figure can be a little higher if the fund actively trades securities or buys overseas stocks and bonds. High-expense ratios cost money.

You should avoid funds with expense ratios of two percent or above. Bond-fund expense ratios average about .75 percent and money funds .50 percent; avoid funds that rack up greater expenses if their returns are not superior.

- Look at the fund's portfolio turnover rate. A rate of 100 percent means that by the end of a year a portfolio manager possessed a totally different stock portfolio from the one that he or she began the year with. Most aggressive funds experience high portfolio turnover because they constantly cash in securities and reap profits. Conservative stock funds tend to buy and hold. You can tell by the portfolio turnover whether or not the fund manager is investing effectively and meeting his or her objectives. If a fund outperformed the market averages and enjoyed a high turnover, the manager was a successful stock picker. If the manager had high portfolio turnover and a poor return, his or her stock selection missed the mark.

- Scrutinize the fund's holdings. What kind of stocks or bonds is the manager buying? What kind of industries are being invested in? You want your stock and bond funds to be broadly diversified, both in individual issues and in industries. Look at the top-ten holdings of the fund and investigate the securities, using the Value Line Investment Survey to check on company profitability and future earnings potential. For bond funds, check the *Standard & Poor's Bond and Stock Guides*. These publications list important data on the financial strength of the company and tell whether a firm can pay back principal and interest on its debt.

If you are allocating, you should be sure to avoid equity mutual funds that have a policy of switching between cash and stocks. Such funds would disrupt your

124

allocation mix. If the fund positioned 30 percent of its assets in cash because the fund manager is bearish and you already placed 20 percent of your investment in money funds, your risk-return parameters would be thrown out of sync.

You want to invest in stock funds that follow a policy of staying fully invested—or nearly so—in stocks.

You also should check the average maturity of the bond funds. You do not want to invest in a bond fund that can move from short maturities to long-term bonds. Rather, seek out a consistent maturity of at least between 10 and 20 years. Widely divergent maturities could mean the portfolio manager is using bond market–timing tactics to attempt to boost the return on the fund. With that strategy, you could become either a big winner or a big loser. Instead, you want a bond fund with a consistent return and a tight margin of error.

NARROWING THE FIELD

Picking the right funds for diversification can be over-whelming. Several easy ways, however, narrow the field before you select the appropriate investment. In chapter 7, we will show you how you can mix more aggressive high-beta mutual funds with lower-risk funds to obtain long-term growth with the least amount of risk.

If you want to keep your asset allocation simple and invest in only one type of low-risk stock fund, consider low-volatility all-weather mutual funds. These are funds that have a track record of solid returns based on the riskiness of their investments. They've registered the best returns per unit of risk over the past ten years ending March 1989.

Table 5.1 shows list the best performing funds over several periods. No one knows what the future might bring. But look for funds that have been top performers over 10 years, plus the last 3 or 5 years.

Table 5.1   Best Managed Stock Funds
Annual Rate of Return %

For the Year Ended 5/31/93		For the 5 Years Ended 5/31/93		For the 10 Years Ended 5/31/93	

Long-Term Growth

Fund	Ret.%	Fund	Ret.%	Fund	Ret.%
PBHG Growth Fund Inc.	52.4	Vista Growth & Income	29.8	CGM Capital Development	19.5
Shearson Special Equities B	44.7	Fidelity Adv Eq Port-Gr Inst	27.1	Fidelity Magellan Fund	17.5
Putnam New Opportunities A	40.5	Fidelity Contrafund	26.8	New York Venture Fund	17.0
AIM Aggressive Growth FD(C)	37.0	CGM Capital Development	26.2	Fidelity Contrafund	16.8
CGM Capital Development	31.7	Berger One Hundred	25.8	Fidelity Destiny Fund I	16.5
Heartland Value Fund	30.5	Janus Fd Inc-Twenty	24.2	Guardian Park Avenue Fund	16.3
Brandywine Blue Fund	29.9	Fidelity Growth Company	22.6	Merrill Lynch Phoenix A	15.8
Cowen Opportunity Fund	29.7	Fidelity Blue Chip Growth	22.1	Fidelity Growth Company	15.5
Strong Common Stock	29.6	AIM Value Fund(C)	21.5	SteinRoe Special Fund	15.3
New Economy Fund (The)	28.4	PBHG Growth Fund Inc.	21.0	FPA Capital Fund	15.3

Growth and Current Income

Fund	Ret.%	Fund	Ret.%	Fund	Ret.%
Main Street Income & Growth	40.8	Main Street Income & Growth	24.7	Financial Industrial Income	16.1
RBB Equity Gr & Income	34.8	FAM Value Fund	18.9	Lexington Corp Leaders B	15.9
UST Master Income & Growth	28.0	IDS Managed Retirement	18.1	Mutual Qualified Fund	15.8
Oppenheimer Total Return A	24.9	Fidelity Growth & Income	18.0	Selected American Shares	15.7
SAFECO Equity Fund	22.5	Financial Industrial Income	18.0	Mutual Shares Fund	15.6
Olympus Growth Fund	22.4	Monetta Fund	17.8	Dodge & Cox Stock Fund	15.5
Mutual Beacon Fund	22.1	Harbor Fund-Capital Apprec	17.5	FPA Paramount Fund	15.4
National Stock Fund	21.8	Dreman High Return Portfolio	17.4	Vanguard Windsor Fund	15.4
Muhlenkamp Fund	21.1	MainStay Value Fund	17.3	Fundamental Investors, Inc	15.3
First American-Special Equity	20.9	Berger One Hundred and One	17.1	Washington Mutual Investors Fd	15.2

Asset Allocation

Fund	Ret.%	Fund	Ret.%	Fund	Ret.%
Valley Forge Fund	18.9	Pasadena Balanced Return Fund	15.2	IAA Trust Asset Allocation Fd	10.1
MetLife-State St. Mgd Assets	18.6	Conn Mutual-Total Return	14.4	Stralem Fund	8.0
Fidelity Asset Manager	16.0	Shearson Eq-Strategic Invest B	12.9	Valley Forge Fund	8.0
Crabbe Huson Asset Allocation	15.8	MIMLIC Asset Allocation	12.7		
Overland Express Asset Alloc	14.9	Fortis Advantage-Asset Alloc	12.4		
J. Hancock Asset Allocation	14.8	Elfun Diversified Fund	12.4		
Prudential Flexi-Conserv A	14.7	Seafirst Asset Allocation	11.9		
Vanguard Asset Allocation	14.2	Stagecoach Asset Allocation	11.8		
Conn Mutual-Total Return	14.1	Overland Express Asset Alloc	11.5		
Prudential Flexi-Conserv B	13.7	Prudential Flexi-Conserv B	11.4		

Balanced

Fund	Ret.%	Fund	Ret.%	Fund	Ret.%
Greenspring Fund	21.2	State Farm Balanced Fund	17.0	CGM Mutual Fund	15.9
Eclipse Balanced Fund	19.7	CGM Mutual Fund	15.9	Phoenix Balanced Fund	14.7
IDS Diversified Equity Income	19.6	Fidelity Balanced Fund	14.7	State Farm Balanced Fund	14.7
CGM Mutual Fund	18.8	Delaware Grp-Delaware Fund	14.4	Dodge & Cox Balanced Fund	14.1
USAA Cornerstone Fund	18.2	Phoenix Balanced Fund	13.9	IDS Mutual Fund	13.7
Fidelity Balanced Fund	18.0	Dodge & Cox Balanced Fund	13.8	MFS Total Return Fund	13.7
Dodge & Cox Balanced Fund	16.2	Equitable Balanced B	13.4	Vanguard Wellington Fund	13.7
Pacifica Balanced Fund	15.3	MFS Total Return Fund	13.2	American Balanced Fund, Inc.	13.3
Kemper Retirement Fund-III	14.9	American Balanced Fund, Inc.	12.9	Sentinel Balanced Fund	13.0
IDS Mutual Fund	14.8	American AAdvantage Balanced Fd	12.7	Alliance Balanced Shares A	12.7

Equity Income

Fund	Ret.%	Fund	Ret.%	Fund	Ret.%
Pioneer Equity Income	21.8	United Income Fund	15.3	United Income Fund	16.2
Prudential Equity Income A	20.8	CoreFund Equity Index Fund	14.7	State Bond Diversified Fd	13.1
Prudential Equity Income B	19.8	USAA Mutual-Income Stock	14.5	Fidelity Adv Eq Port-Inc Inst	13.0
Royce Fund-Equity Income	19.5	Shearson Premium Total Return B	14.4	Delaware Grp-Decatur Fd I	13.0
Fidelity Adv Eq Port-Inc Inst	18.8	American AAdvantage Equity Fund	14.4	Fidelity Equity Income	13.0
Stratton Monthly Dividend	18.5	Capital Income Builder, Inc.	14.0	Stratton Monthly Dividend	13.0
Fidelity Equity Income	18.4	Franklin Inv-Specl Eq Incm	13.6	SAFECO Income Fund	12.7
MetLife-State St. Eq Income	18.1	Prudential Equity Income B	13.5	Smith Barney Fds-Inc & Gr A	12.4
Franklin Inv-Specl Eq Incm	17.6	Stratton Monthly Dividend	13.3	Mairs & Power Income Fund	12.2
PFAMCo Small Cap Value Fund	16.8	US Income Fund	13.1	Oppenheimer Equity Income	12.2

CDA/Wiesenberger Mutual Funds Update

In addition to low-volatility stock funds that move from fixed-income investments into stocks, several other asset-allocating funds are available to investors. These funds invest in several classes of assets, such as stocks, bonds, precious metals, foreign securities, and cash. Thus, they do your asset-allocating for you. We will discuss these funds later in the book.

Whether you are investing in an all-weather equity fund or in several different types of funds, before you invest you should do the following:

- Determine how much risk you are willing to take based on your financial needs and goals.
- Decide which types of funds you want to invest in. If you want more growth, you will need to invest in aggressive- or growth-stock funds. If you want to play it a little safer, invest in growth and income funds. Do you want to hedge your portfolio against inflation by investing in precious-metals funds? Do you want to create an income cushion and hedge against stock declines by investing in bond funds? Finally, do you want to anchor your portfolio in money funds?
- Narrow your investment choices to the funds with the most consistent performance.
- Make sure you invest in no-load mutual-funds families with a stable of funds to choose from. Make sure you have telephone-exchange privileges.

One excellent source of information on mutual-funds returns, risk and other important criteria is the *Morningstar Mutual Funds,* mentioned previously. This quarterly directory lists portfolio holdings, risk-return rankings, ten-year performance records, and tollfree telephone numbers for more than 1,100 mutual funds.

Table 5.2 shows the best performing bond funds over the past ten years. You don't want to own high yielding

Table 5.2 Best Managed Bond Funds
Annual Rate of Return %

For the Year Ended 5/31/93		For the 5 Years Ended 5/31/93		For the 10 Years Ended 5/31/93	

Flexible Income

Fund	Ret.%	Fund	Ret.%	Fund	Ret.%
Pacific Horizon Capital Inc	27.5	Fidelity Convertible Securities	19.1	Fidelity Puritan Fund	14.5
Rochester Fd Series-Bd Fd Grwth	25.3	Pacific Horizon Capital Inc	18.7	Lindner Dividend Fund	14.1
Fidelity Convertible Securities	22.7	Liberty Equity Income Fund	14.3	National Income & Growth A	13.9
MainStay Convertible Fund	22.2	Fidelity Puritan Fund	14.3	Vanguard Wellesley Income Fd	13.9
Fidelity Capital & Income	21.0	Lindner Dividend Fund	14.2	Income Fund of America, Inc (The)	13.6
Franklin Inv-Convert Secs	20.7	National Income & Growth A	14.1	Fidelity Capital & Income	13.2
Fidelity Puritan Fund	20.7	MainStay Convertible Fund	14.0	Franklin Income Fund	13.0
Lindner Dividend Fund	19.9	Berwyn Income Fund	14.0	Seligman Income Fund A	12.3
Putnam Convertible Inc & Gth	19.1	Vanguard Wellesley Income Fd	13.9	USAA Mutual-Income Fund	12.2
Vanguard Convertible Fund	18.4	United Retirement Shares	13.9	Phoenix Convertible Fund	12.0

Corporate Bond

Fund	Ret.%	Fund	Ret.%	Fund	Ret.%
Alliance Bond-Corporate Bond A	25.5	Alliance Bond-Corporate Bond A	13.6	Alliance Bond-Corporate Bond A	12.3
Loomis Sayles Bond Fund	17.6	Vanguard Fixed-Inv Grade	13.4	FPA New Income Fund	12.0
Westcore Long-Term Bond	17.4	SEI Instl Managed-Bond	13.2	Vanguard Fixed-Inv Grade	11.9
National Multi-Sector Fixed A	16.9	PIMCO Total Return Fund	12.9	Bond Fund of America, Inc (The)	11.9
SEI Instl Managed-Bond	16.8	Shearson Investment Grade Bd B	12.6	Shearson Investment Grade Bd B	11.8
Vanguard Fixed-Inv Grade	15.9	Harbor Fund-Bond	12.5	Elfun Income Fund	11.8
Putnam Diversified Income A	15.8	Dreyfus Strategic Income	12.5	IDS Bond Fund	11.6
Sierra Tr Corporate Income	15.2	FPA New Income Fund	12.1	GE S&S Long Term Bond	11.6
Bond Fund of America, Inc (The)	15.1	Bond Port. for Endowments, Inc.	12.1	Bond Port. for Endowments, Inc.	11.6
Strong Government Securities	15.0	IDS Bond Fund	11.9	United Bond Fund	11.4

Corporate High Yield

Fund	Ret.%	Fund	Ret.%	Fund	Ret.%
PaineWebber High Income A	22.3	Fidelity Adv High Yield Port	17.1	Kemper High Yield Fund	12.8
Keystone America Strategic Incm	21.8	Kemper Inv Port-Divers Inc	14.7	Merrill Lynch Corp Bd-Hi Inc A	12.8
Venture Income Plus	19.6	Oppenheimer Champion Hi Yield	14.6	AIM High Yield Fund(C)	12.6
Keystone B-4	19.1	Kemper Diversified Income	14.1	Liberty High Income Bond	12.4
Advantage High Yield Bond	19.0	Merrill Lynch Corp Bd-Hi Inc A	14.1	Eaton Vance Inc Fd of Boston	12.3
Dean Witter High Yield Sec	18.9	Liberty High Income Bond	13.8	Colonial High Yield Secs A	12.0
National Bond Fund	18.8	PaineWebber High Income A	13.6	Putnam High Yield Trust A	11.2
MetLife-State St. High Inc	18.4	American High-Income Trust	13.2	Northeast Investors Trust	11.2
Shearson High Income Bond B	18.4	AIM High Yield Fund(C)	12.7	Vanguard Fixed-High Yield	11.0
MainStay High Yield Corp Bond	18.1	IDEX II High Yield Portfolio	12.4	Phoenix High Yield Fd	10.8

Government Mortgage-Backed

Fund	Ret.%	Fund	Ret.%	Fund	Ret.%
Managers Interm Mortgage Sec Fd	18.7	Managers Interm Mortgage Sec Fd	13.6	Vanguard Fixed-GNMA	11.4
Heartland US Government	18.5	Heartland US Government	12.1	Federated GNMA-Inst Shares	11.1
CA Invest Tr-US Government	15.5	CA Invest Tr-US Government	11.7	Lexington GNMA Income Fund	10.3
U.S. Government Fund	12.5	Princor Govt Securities Income	11.5	Prudential GNMA Fund B	9.7
Alliance Mortgage Securities A	11.5	Vanguard Fixed-GNMA	11.5	SunAmerica Federal Securities	9.7
Dreyfus Inv GNMA LP	11.4	Smith Barney Fds-Mthly Pay A	11.5		
Alliance Mortgage Securities B	10.9	SEI Cash+Plus Tr-GNMA	11.3		
Princor Govt Securities Income	10.8	Federated GNMA-Inst Shares	11.3		
USAA GNMA Trust	10.7	Benham Govt Income-GNMA	11.1		
Franklin Partners-Tax Adv USG	10.6	Wright Current Income Fund	11.1		

Government Securities

Fund	Ret.%	Fund	Ret.%	Fund	Ret.%
PIMCO Long Term US Govt	20.5	Scudder US Govt Zero-2000	14.4	Kemper US Govt Sec	11.2
Piper Jaffray Inst'l Government	20.3	Vanguard Fixed-Long Trm US Tres	12.9	Lord Abbett US Gov Securities	11.0
Scudder US Govt Zero-2000	19.6	Dreyfus 100% UST Long	12.7	Value Line US Gov Securities	10.9
Loomis Sayles US Govt Sec	17.1	Rushmore-US Gov't Long Term	12.2	Fidelity Gov Securities	10.6
Vanguard Fixed-Long Trm US Tres	16.9	Voyageur US Gov Securities	11.6	Composite US Government Secs	10.4
Dreyfus 100% UST Long	16.9	Smith Barney Fds-US Govt A	11.4	Franklin US Govt Securities	10.3
Advantage Government Sec	16.8	Colonial Federal Secs A	11.4	Federated Inc Tr-Inst Shares	10.3
Rushmore-US Gov't Long Term	16.3	Rushmore-US Gov't Intermed	11.3	Mutual of Omaha America	10.1
Stagecoach US Gov Alloc	16.0	Chubb Government Securities	11.3	Fund For US Govt Securities	10.0
Rightime Govt Secs Fund	15.6	Overland Express US Govt Inc	11.2	Benham Treasury Note Trust	9.9

CDA/Wiesenberger Mutual Funds Update

funds and watch your principal decline in value. These funds have shown the best returns in market value plus yield.

COUNT YOUR MUTUAL FUNDS

Over the years, we have reviewed countless mutual fund portfolios for individual investors. One of the more common mistakes these investors make is investing in too many mutual funds. And holding too many mutual funds can be harmful to your long-run financial health.

We can understand why investors end up owning too many funds. First, most seasoned investors know that portfolio diversification reduces risk. As we have demonstrated elsewhere, a 30-stock portfolio contains about one-third the risk of a single stock portfolio and no less return potential. Second, most mutual fund investors make their selections on the basis of recent past returns. Since the top performing group of funds changes from year-to-year, return-chasing investors end up buying a lot of funds. Most of the time these investors fail to purge their portfolios of yesterday's fallen stars and end up with a growing list of funds. Finally, the financial press tends to glorify top performing mutual fund managers in glowing articles. Investors take these articles as endorsements of future performance potential and seek to jump on the band wagon.

HOW MANY FUNDS?

How many funds should an investor own? Of course, it depends. However, one fund is certainly not enough and more than a dozen is probably too many. Although diversification is beneficial, there is a limit to the benefits of diversification. Hold a dozen funds and you have indirectly invested in hundreds of stocks. Adding another fund rarely reduces investment risk further. On the other hand, holding too many funds can erode long-run investment returns. Here's why.

Funds with similar investment objectives and management style frequently invest in the same stocks. In fact, when we examined the portfolios of a number of popular equity funds we found that these funds had invested from one-quarter to one-half of their assets in the stocks of the same companies. The danger in holding funds with common investments is that when one portfolio manager deems it appropriate to buy more shares another portfolio manager may deem it appropriate to lighten up on the same stock. As a result, the shareholder of these funds assumes the brokerage commissions for the sale by one portfolio manager and the purchase by the other. In other words, after these transactions, the mutual fund shareholder's portfolio remains unchanged. However, the portfolio's return is reduced by the payment of redundant transactions costs. And the probability of this occurring is enhanced the greater the number of funds that are held.

Since the appropriate number of mutual funds to hold depends on an investors objective, we have based our recommendations on four investment strategies: growth, growth and income, income, and asset allocation.

STRATEGIES

Growth Investors with long investment horizons should seek capital appreciation primarily and disregard the stock market's short-term swings. This implies a portfolio dominated by equity funds. However, given that blue-chip stocks, small-cap stocks, and international equities exhibit returns that are less than perfectly correlated with one another, growth-oriented investors can reduce risk by including all three categories of funds in their portfolio. As a consequence, proper diversification requires that growth-seeking investors spread their investments across five or six equity funds in addition to a money market fund, which can be used to park temporary cash. These funds should include: small-cap growth, small-cap value, large-cap growth, large-cap value, international equity, and perhaps a specialty fund such as a regional international fund or an industry sector fund.

Growth and Income Investors. Because of their desire for some current income, growth and income investors' portfolios should be more narrowly defined than those of growth investors. Typically, growth and income investors will hold both conservative (income producing) stock funds and bond funds. The recommended portfolio should include: a balanced fund, an equity income fund, a large-cap value fund, and perhaps two bond funds (a corporate and government bond fund). Including a money market fund, the ideal growth and income portfolio will contain five or six funds.

Income Investors. Since the returns of bond funds tend to be much more highly correlated with one another, the income-seeking investor needs to hold fewer funds that the growth-seeking investor. However, income investors should diversify their portfolios among corporate, government, and international bond funds. Add a money market fund, and income investors can obtain a high degree of diversification with as few as four funds.

Asset Allocation Investors. Asset allocators attempt to minimize forecasting errors by investing in many categories of assets. The goal is to produce a low-variability portfolio. We recommend that these investors invest in funds drawn from seven asset categories including: small-cap stocks, blue-chip stocks, domestic bonds, international bonds, international stocks, gold, and money market funds. In addition, asset allocators should divide their small and large-cap investments between value and growth funds and their domestic bond funds among corporate and government. Thus, asset allocators can hold as many as a dozen funds without having to worry about the return erosion that occurs when investments overlap.

DON'T BUY EVERYTHING

Avoid becoming a mutual fund junkie. Establish concrete investment objectives and invest in only those funds that will make a meaningful contribution to your long-range plan. Eliminate redundancy and increase your return potential by investing in an appropriate number of mutual funds. Periodically, conduct an audit of your mutual fund portfolio. Classify each fund by investment objective and management style. Eliminate funds with overlapping objectives and styles. When making a new fund selection, determine which fund will be sold to accommodate the new purchase. Follow this advice and you will increase both the efficiency and long-run return potential of your mutual fund portfolio.

CHAPTER 6

Model Mutual-Funds Portfolios

We have talked about diversification, asset allocation and assessing your risk level to match your investments. Now let's look at some model portfolios that you can use to allocate assets.

For the investor who has at least $10,000, mutual funds are the easiest route to a stable portfolio. They provide professional management, diversification and a wide choice of funds to pick from. Individuals who like to conduct their own research and can invest at least $50,000 to $100,000, however, can allocate assets with individual stocks and bonds.

MUTUAL-FUNDS FRONT-RUNNERS

Here are several suggested mutual-funds portfolios for the low-, moderate- and higher-risk investor. The funds

ADDISON PUBLIC LIBRARY
ADDISON, ILLINOIS

selected are no-load, with long-term records that provide the best returns per unit of risk as well as the best returns in up and down markets in their respective fund categories.

First, we will list the model portfolios and then we will profile the funds. Model portfolios are designed to provide guidelines for the construction of actual portfolios of investments. Each one offers a certain level of risk and return to match individual investment objectives.

The *aggressive portfolio* is designed to achieve maximum capital appreciation. This riskier-than-average portfolio is best suited to individuals with long-term investment horizons—young couples or single individuals who want to build their wealth to meet long-term investment needs.

The *moderately aggressive portfolio* is less volatile than the aggressive portfolio, but the return will be lower. This portfolio will build wealth for those who do not want to take so much risk. The funds in this portfolio should be held for at least five years.

The *growth-and-income portfolio* gives investors a more-balanced asset-allocation mix. It is designed to yield more than a T-bill would and outpace the rate of inflation. It is suited for investors who are in their peak earning years—investors who already have accumulated wealth and want to preserve the purchasing power of their money.

The *income portfolio* is designed for investors who want current income without taking any risks. This portfolio is best suited for retired people who need current income to meet daily expenses.

The *all-weather portfolio* is invested in securities worldwide and precious metals for diversification. This portfolio is about one-third less volatile than the U.S. stock market and acts as a hedge when one type of financial market is performing poorly.

AGGRESSIVE PORTFOLIO MIX

The investor looking to build wealth who can handle risk in return for potential long-term reward should consider the following funds:

Acorn International	10%
Columbia Special	17%
Financial European	10%
Founders Discovery	20%
Vanguard Small Cap	16%
Money Funds	27%

MODERATELY AGGRESSIVE MIX

For growth with a little less risk, investors should consider the following funds:

Acorn International	15%
Lindner Fund	11%
T. Rowe Price Equity Income Fund	22%
Vanguard Small Cap	19%
Money Funds	33%

GROWTH AND INCOME MIX

Investors who want a more balanced portfolio to preserve their wealth and purchasing power should consider the following funds:

Babson Value	10%
Bartlett Basic Value	10%
Financial Industrial Income	18%
Lindner Fund	10%
T. Rowe Price Equity Income Fund	12%
Vanguard Small Cap	10%
Money Funds	30%

INCOME MIX

Investors seeking current income and low risk should consider the following funds:

Benham T-Note Trust	17%
Lexington Gold	5%
Safeco Income	13%
T. Rowe Price International Bond	11%
T. Rowe Price Equity Income Fund	10%
Vanguard Short-term Cap	19%
Money Funds	32%

ALL-WEATHER PORTFOLIOS

Investors who want to split up investments to minimize losses if, for example, the U.S. stock and bond markets perform poorly, can include gold and overseas investments. They also can change the mix of their investments to meet their risk tolerance.

GENERIC ASSET-ALLOCATION PORTFOLIO

The generic all-weather portfolio for those who want to buy and hold, or dollar-cost-average their investments for the long term, include the following funds:

Vanguard Small Cap	13%
Lexington Gold	5%
Vanguard Index 500	11%
Vanguard World	10%
T. Rowe Price International Bond	15%
Benham T-Note Trust	19%
Money Funds	27%

LOW-RISK ASSET-ALLOCATION PORTFOLIO

Investors who want to lower their risk level and allocate assets can weight the mix more heavily with money funds and less heavily with more aggressive stock funds. Based on the LaPorte Assets Allocation software, such a portfolio would include the following:

Lindner Fund	20%
Partners Fund	7%
Mutual Beacon	8%
Fidelity Intermediate Bond	4%
T. Rowe Price International Bond	29%
Money Funds	32%

MODERATE-RISK ASSET-ALLOCATION PORTFOLIO

Those who are willing to risk losing about 8 percent to 10 percent in any given year, in return for longer-term gains should consider the following funds:

Janus Fund	10%
Lindner Fund	16%
Partners Fund	16%
20th Century Growth	15%
Mutual Beacon	15%
U.S. Gold	3%
Money Funds	25%

HIGHER-RISK CAPITAL-APPRECIATION ALLOCATION PORTFOLIO

Investors who are willing to hold for long-term growth with a good shot at outperforming the market should consider this mix of funds. Be forewarned. You could see the market value of your portfolio drop 15 percent or more in any given year:

Janus Fund	11%
Stein Roe Special Fund	12%
Lindner Fund	15%
Partners Fund	14%
Fidelity Growth Company	15%
Mutual Beacon	15%
U.S. Gold	8%
T. Rowe Price International Bond	9%

FUND PROFILES

Here is a specific look at the recommended funds, how they invest and what their yield histories have been. These funds, which have been consistent performers, should make good long-term investment vehicles.

Acorn International Fund. This is a new fund with a lot of promise. Fund manager Ralph Wagner gained his reputation managing the Acorn Fund. The Acorn Fund is unfortunately closed to new investors. But it grew at an annual rate of over 16 percent over the past ten years ended in March 1993.

The Acorn International Fund relies on Wagner's stock picking style. He invests in undervalued small- and mid-sized stocks overseas. At least 75 percent of the fund is invested abroad. This year-to-date ended in March 1993, the fund is up an impressive 16.5 percent. The fund is no load and carries no 12b-1 fee. The minimum initial and subsequent investments are $500 and $100.

Babson Value. This is a solid growth and income that buys undervalued stocks. The fund manager wants to own low p/e stocks of firms with strong balance sheets and profitability. The fund is well diversified across a number of industries and owns out-of-favor stocks that should perform well when the economy improves. Over the past five years ended in March 1993, the fund grew at an annual rate of 11.24 percent. The fund is no load and carries no 12b-1 fee. The minimum initial and subsequent investments are $1,000 and $100.

Bartlett Basic Value. This is another growth and income fund that buys undervalued stocks. The fund manager buys large company stocks when they are underpriced. He profits when the firms' earnings improve and other investors jump on the bandwagon. The fund grew at a 10.2 percent annual rate over the past ten years ended in March 1993. The fund is no load

and carries no 12b-1 fee. The minimum initial and subsequent investments are $5,000 and $100.

Benham Treasury Note Fund.   This is a well managed short-term Government bond fund. It yields about
75 percent of the long bond rate, but is half as risky.
Over the past five years ended in March 1993, the fund
gained 9.7 percent as interest rates declined. This is no
load and carries no 12b-1 fee. The minimum initial and
subsequent investments are $1,000 and $100.

Columbia Special Fund.   This is a top notch aggressive stock fund. The fund manager buys undervalued
stocks and growth stocks depending on the outlook for
the market and the economy. Over the past five years
ended in March 1993, the fund gained 18.93 percent
annually. This is a no-load and no 12b-1 fund. The minimum initial and subsequent investments in the fund are
$2,000 and $100.

Founders Discovery Fund.   This is a top performing
small company stock fund. The fund manager buys
growth stocks or firms with earnings that are growing
faster the S&P 500, the economy and inflation. Over the
past five years ended in March 1993, the fund grew at
an annual rate of 25.8 percent. This is a no-load and no
12b-1 fund. The minimum initial and subsequent investments are $1,000 and $100.

Invesco Industrial Income Fund.   This is a conservative stock fund that sports one of the best risk adjusted
rates of return of all equity funds on the market. The
fund invests in larger companies in industries that will
perform well. The fund also owns high yielding stocks for
income. Over the past ten years ended in March 1993,
the fund grew at an annual rate of 15.95 percent. This is
a no-load and no 12b-1 fund. The minimum initial and
subsequent investments are $1,000 and $50.

Lexington Gold Fund.   If you own one precious metals fund, this is the one to buy. All precious metals funds
are volatile. Lexington, however, is one of the best man-

age funds in its category. The fund owns precious metals mining stocks and should serve as a good inflation hedge in any portfolio. Over the past year ended in March 1993, the fund gained 20.6 percent. This is a no-load and no 12b-1 fund. The minimum initial and subsequent investments are $1,000 and $50.

Lindner Fund. This is a well managed growth fund that buys undervalued stocks both here and abroad. The fund manager looks for special situations. He wants to own firms with over look asset values. If the manager can't find undervalued companies, he goes to cash. The fund should be considered a core holding in any portfolio. The fund gained 13.3 percent annually over the past ten years ended in March 1993. This is a no-load and no 12b-1 fund. Minimum initial and subsequent investments are $2,000 and $100.

Safeco Income. This is an excellent all weather fund. The fund invests in both stocks and bonds for the long term. You will earn about 80 percent of the return on the S&P 500 with about half the risk when you invest in the Safeco Income Fund. Over the past ten years the fund grew at a 12.75 percent annual rate. The fund owns a lot of high dividend yield utility and blue-chip stocks. This is a no-load and no 12b-1 fund. The minimum initial and subsequent investments are $1,000 and $100.

T. Rowe Price International Bond Fund. This is one of the best run overseas bond funds available. Now the fund is profiting from declining interest rates in Europe. However, the fund out-yields U.S. funds by more than one percent. Over the past five years ended in March 1993 the fund gained 8 percent.

T. Rowe Price Equity Income Fund. This is a fund that invests in high dividend yield stocks for long-term growth. It owns Dow and S&P 500 stocks as well as overseas equities. The fund also invests in bonds and preferred stocks. Over the past five years ended in March 1993, the fund gained 12.5 percent. This is a no-load and no 12b-1 fund. The minimum initial and subsequent investments are $2,500 and $100.

Vanguard Index 500. This is an index fund that matches the return on the S&P 500 stock market index. This fund should be considered a core holding. It is one of the lowest cost stock funds on the market. The expense ratio is just .19 percent. The fund outperforms more than 50 percent of all other growth and income funds. Over the past ten years ended in March 1993, the fund gained 14.04 percent annually. This is a no-load and no 12b-1 fund. The minimum initial and subsequent investments are $3,000 and $100.

Vanguard Short-Term Bond Fund Corporate. This fund invests in investment grade short-term bonds. The fund's expenses are low and you get a 5 percent yield.

Vanguard Small Capitalization Stock Fund. This is an over-the-counter small company stock fund. Like other Vanguard funds it is low cost and should be considered a core holding. Over the past three years ended in March 1993, the fund gained 14.84 percent annually.

Vanguard World-U.S. Growth. This is a well managed growth fund that invests for capital gains. The fund buys undervalued stocks with strong earnings. Over the past ten years ended in March 1993, the fund grew at a 12.2 percent annual rate. This is a no-load and no 12b-1 fund. The minimum initial and subsequent investments are $3,000 and $100.

DON'T RULE OUT OTHER NO-LOAD FUNDS

There are other well managed funds you should consider. The funds above are just a few to be considered. Check out other no-load fund families. Write the 100 percent No-Load Mutual Fund Council at 1501 Broadway, Suite 312, New York, New York 10036. Inquire about their directory of funds.

CHAPTER 7

How to Evaluate Performance

Now that you have a diversified portfolio, how can you tell if your investment strategy is working? You cannot just compare a mix of stocks, bonds, metals, money funds, and real estate with the performance of the Dow Jones Industrial Average or the S&P 500—your portfolio is a different type of organism altogether.

Asset-allocated portfolios are safer than these indexes, for one thing. You will not outperform the stock market during a bull market, but you will not tumble with it during a bear market, either. Even though you split up your investments among different types of individual securities or mutual funds, however, you still face several dangers. Here are a few cautionary notes:

- First, sometimes all classes of assets lose money at the same time. You could conceivably be holding on to a growth-stock mutual fund, a bond fund, and a gold fund that all decline in price at the same time.

- Second, if you split up the total too evenly among different assets, losses and gains could be equal—a result known as a washout—over the long term. You could end up squeezing out a minimal return comparable to that of a passbook savings account.
- Third, you may lose opportunity if you invest too little in stocks and the market goes into a sustained rally.

THE SECRET OF VALUE-ADDED GAIN

You really cannot compare apples to oranges. Your portfolio is safer than the stock market, so you will not rack up huge gains overnight even if the market does. One way to judge allocation performance is to apply a simple technique that pension-fund portfolio managers have been using for years. Figure the value-added gain of your portfolio—how your specific mix performs compared to several benchmark indicators. These might include T-bills or a fixed percentage of stocks and bonds based on the S&P 500 and Salomon Brothers Corporate Bond Index.

"My value-added gain on my portfolio was five percent last year" is a fancy way of saying that your diversified portfolio did better than a benchmark index that measures the performance of diversified portfolios. Forget about measures such as the Dow, which are impossible to keep up with all the time without compromising the safety of your assets.

QUICK AND EASY WAY

Here's a quick and easy way to see how your investments are performing. Check a copy of *Barron's* every three months when it publishes the quarterly data on mutual funds. Look at the section that lists the mutual-funds performance categories computed by Lipper

Analytical Services. A certain section shows the percentage gain, with reinvestment of dividends, of stock, bond, and other types of mutual funds. We are assuming that the average performance of all stock, bond, or gold funds will be a close approximation of the market averages in those categories.

Then calculate the total return on your investments. If you do not want to perform all these calculations and you are heavily allocated with mutual funds, you can read several newsletters that list specific mutual funds and index total returns (see the appendix). You also could go to the public library and check the *CDA / Wiesenberger's Investment Company Service, Standard & Poor's Stock Guide* and *The Mutual Fund Source Book*. For individual stocks and bonds, you also can check *Standard & Poor's Stock and Bond Guides*.

Remember that the gain includes the price appreciation of the security and the reinvestment of dividends and/or capital gains in new shares. You will have to check the most recent statement from your mutual fund to see how many shares and at what price per share, or net asset value, distributions were reinvested. For individual securities you can look at your purchase price and figure the gain or loss compared to the market value at the end of the time period you are using.

Assume you bought a stock at $10 per share and a year later it is at $12. The gain is (12 divided by 10) – 1 or 1.2 – 1, which equals .20 or a 20-percent gain. If the current price is $8, then 8 divided by 10 equals 80 percent less 1, giving you a 20-percent loss. In addition, if the dividend yield when you acquired the stock was 3 percent, add that to the 20-percent increase in price to get your total return of 23 percent. If you lost 20 percent, the return will actually be down only 17 percent because of the 3 percent distribution.

Mutual funds are a little different because dividends and capital gains can be reinvested in new shares. You will have to calculate the total return this way: If you invested $3,000 in 100 shares of ABC Equity Income Fund at $30 a share and you reinvested dividends of $1.20 per share at $32, this equals $120 in dividend income, divided by the current price of $32. This calculation equals 3.75 new shares. Your total number of shares is now 103.75. At the end of the quarter, the market value of your investment is now $35 per share. The value of your investment is now 103.75 shares multiplied by $35 or $3,631.25. Your total return or percentage gain with reinvestment is 21.04 percent.

Next compare the return on your allocated portfolio with that of the Lipper indexes that are listed in *Barron's* every week. Calculate the percentage gain on your total investment and subtract that from the performance of the same amount in your benchmarks. Let's posit a blended portfolio with 30 percent in an aggressive-stock fund, 10 percent in a growth and income fund, 42 percent in an international fund, 12 percent in a gold fund, and 6 percent in a money fund. How did it do (see Table 7.1)?

For example, your aggressive stock fund gained 14 percent over the past 12 months. Your growth and income fund gained 18.5 percent, the international fund which invested in Latin America and the Far East grew 19.6 percent, the gold fund lost 20 percent, and the income fund gained 8 percent. Your actual gain was: .30(14) + .10(18.5) + .42(19.6) + .12(−20) + .06(8) = 12.30 percent.

A 20 percent split against the fund averages in each category in Table 7.1 resulted in a gain of .20(7.49) + .20(9.45) + .20(−3.75) + .20(−15.07) + .20(10.84) = 1.79 percent.

You had one heck of a year. The 12.30 percent increase in your portfolio, minus the 1.79 percent index gain equals a 10.51 percent value added gain, or an extra $105.10 per $1,000, on your asset allocation mix compared to the benchmark.

Table 7.1 Lipper—Mutual Fund Performance Analysis— Performance Summary

12/31/92 T.N.A. ($ mils)	No. of Funds	Type of Fund	Cumulative Total Reinvestment Performance				
			10/11/90 to 1/28/93	7/12/90 to 1/28/93	1/30/92 to 1/28/93	12/31/92 to 1/28/93	1/21/93 to 1/28/93
41,382.7	136	Capital Appreciation Funds	+ 72.29%	+ 32.17%	+ 7.49%	+ 1.44%	- 0.12%
135,806.7	365	Growth Funds	+ 67.73%	+ 31.59%	+ 8.20%	+ 1.13%	+ 0.03%
29,138.8	155	Small Company Growth Funds	+ 97.24%	+ 43.20%	+ 9.53%	+ 2.04%	+ 0.02%
140,224.8	286	Growth & Income Funds	+ 57.61%	+ 29.75%	+ 9.54%	+ 1.05%	+ 0.48%
40,393.8	74	Equity Income Funds	+ 53.36%	+ 30.22%	+ 10.88%	+ 1.31%	+ 0.70%
386,946.8	1016	General Equity Funds Average	+ 68.15%	+ 32.48%	+ 8.89%	+ 1.30%	+ 0.19%
5,359.6	15	Health/Biotechnology Funds	+ 73.38%	+ 45.88%	- 12.52%	- 3.80%	- 0.80%
1,725.3	22	Natural Resources Funds	+ 4.10%	- 2.97%	+ 4.03%	+ 1.51%	+ 3.13%
248.6	8	Environmental Funds	+ 20.99%	- 8.22%	- 9.15%	+ 2.17%	- 0.17%
3,264.1	21	Science & Technology Funds	+111.26%	+ 43.63%	+ 10.61%	+ 3.23%	- 1.85%
1,632.7	27	Specialty/Miscellaneous Funds	+ 74.61%	+ 32.34%	+ 10.33%	+ 2.09%	+ 0.71%
17,310.7	37	Utility Funds	+ 46.69%	+ 39.81%	+ 13.40%	+ 1.36%	+ 0.37%
1,687.0	14	Financial Services Funds	+161.61%	+ 95.50%	+ 36.84%	+ 4.42%	+ 0.94%
341.7	6	Real Estate Funds	+·60.76%	+ 29.56%	+ 11.24%	+ 3.49%	+ 0.33%
130.2	4	Option Income Funds	+ 41.43%	+ 20.32%	+ 8.71%	+ 0.45%	+ 0.73%
2,216.7	33	Gold Oriented Funds	- 18.77%	- 23.39%	- 15.02%	- 0.75%	+ 3.14%
15,946.1	57	Global Funds	+ 21.34%	+ 1.60%	+ 0.89%	+ 1.13%	+ 0.09%
2,586.8	9	Global Small Company Funds	+ 41.59%	+ 11.60%	+ 1.73%	+ 2.88%	+ 0.10%
17,030.6	107	International Funds	+ 8.61%	- 7.87%	- 3.75%	+ 1.10%	+ 0.38%
3,283.9	28	European Region Funds	- 2.06%	- 15.74%	- 6.24%	+ 1.97%	+ 0.43%
2,214.0	24	Pacific Region Funds	+ 14.50%	- 5.72%	+ 1.43%	+ 1.05%	+ 0.15%
701.1	6	Japanese Funds	- 27.21%	- 41.33%	- 17.99%	- 0.71%	+ 1.38%
334.4	4	Latin American Funds	N/A	N/A	- 9.57%	- 1.16%	- 2.19%
51.4	3	Canadian Funds	- 2.00%	- 11.62%	- 4.58%	- 0.01%	+ 1.78%
44,365.0	271	World Equity Funds Average	+ 5.59%	- 9.85%	- 4.58%	+ 0.94%	+ 0.63%
461,324.7	1427	All Equity Funds Average	+ 56.76%	+ 25.12%	+ 6.14%	+ 1.24%	+ 0.29%
10,898.5	69	Flexible Portfolio Funds	+ 49.10%	+ 31.13%	+ 8.92%	+ 1.40%	+ 0.45%
2,672.4	16	Global Flexible Port Funds	+ 26.61%	+ 17.81%	+ 3.60%	+ 1.16%	+ 0.14%
29,701.7	88	Balanced Funds	+ 49.05%	+ 31.87%	+ 9.00%	+ 1.22%	+ 0.51%
907.6	8	Balanced Target Maturity Funds	+ 54.18%	+ 37.18%	+ 9.84%	+ 1.83%	+ 0.55%
2,757.5	26	Convertible Securities Funds	+ 61.43%	+ 37.08%	+ 13.55%	+ 2.29%	+ 0.57%
8,851.2	18	Income Funds	+ 45.87%	+ 34.58%	+ 10.84%	+ 1.51%	+ 0.84%
27,492.5	101	World Income Funds	+ 16.35%	+ 24.39%	+ 3.21%	+ 0.85%	+ 0.44%
280,252.8	789	Fixed Income Funds	+ 35.40%	+ 32.91%	+ 10.38%	+ 1.33%	+ 0.57%
826,545.9	2556	Long-term Taxable Funds					
		Average	+ 49.55%	+ 28.40%	+ 7.74%	+ 1.29%	+ 0.40%
		Median	+ 46.10%	+ 30.40%	+ 9.00%	+ 1.30%	+ 0.50%
		No. of Funds with a % Change	1716	1667	2134	2530	2529

Lipper—Mutual Fund Performance Analysis
Copyright, Lipper Analytical Services, Inc., 1993

Of course this is just a hypothetical example. Your objective is to diversify your investments based on your risk tolerance. You may or may not outperform the average by a wide margin.

Table 7.2 will help you compare your asset allocation mix with the Lipper Fund Averages.

Table 7.2   Asset-Allocation Comparison

Your Investments			Lipper Indexes			
Fund	% Mix	% Return	Class	% Mix	% Return	% Differ
A.						
B.						
C.						
D.						
E.						
Total	____			____	____	____

How did you compare with balanced funds—the funds in which the portfolio manager maintains about a 60/40 stock-and-bond split. Balanced fund gained 9 percent for the year: you received a value added gain of 3.3 percent over this benchmark. You earned an extra $33 per $1,000 with your asset allocation mix compared to balanced funds.

A WORD ABOUT ALL-IN-ONE FUNDS

Wall Street professionals sell people what they want, not what they need. They will sell you whatever investment is hot, even if it is financial futures in the Iranian stock market. When the bull market was raging from 1984 through 1987, everyone wanted growth and big profits, so investment companies and brokerage firms sold growth stocks and go-go mutual funds. When we lost almost half of our gains in October of 1987, what do you think financiers began peddling? Asset allocation and asset-allocation mutual funds.

More than a dozen asset-allocation funds are on the market today, and brokerage firms are heavily promoting all-weather investing. These funds invest across the board: in U.S. and overseas stocks and bonds, precious metals and possibly real estate. Why didn't they tell us about this strategy before the crash?

The three no-load asset-allocation funds that have registered laudable returns based on their level of risk should be considered by investors who want an all-weather stock fund (see Table 7.3). The Fidelity Asset Manager will shift among stocks, bonds, and cash based on the managers outlook for the economy and the markets. The manager also invests overseas. The fund gained 16.2 percent a year over the past three years ended in March 1993. Vanguard's Asset Allocation Fund is also attractive. The fund gained 12.8 percent annually over the past three years ended in March 1993.

The Crabbe Huson Asset Allocation fund is another all-in-one fund. Over the past three years the fund also grew at a 12.3 percent annual rate.

The Permanent Portfolio in Petaluma, California, is the oldest asset-allocation fund on the market. The fund invests fixed percentages in a wide range of assets in order to preserve principal and purchasing power. Over the previous five years, however, the fund has registered an annual compound rate of just five percent and barely kept pace with the rate of inflation.

Each of these asset-allocation funds differs in how it maintains the investment mix. The Blanchard fund is more growth-oriented, the Cornerstone fund takes a middle-of-the-road approach, and the Permanent Portfolio is a very conservative fund.

More and more asset-allocation funds are coming to the market. But they are not all alike. The funds men-

Table 7.3   Asset Allocation Funds

Asset Allocation / Fund	This Month Pcnt	Rnk	1993 To Date Pcnt	Rnk	Latest 12 Months Pcnt	Rnk	Annualized Total Return Thru 5/31/93 3 Years Pcnt	Rnk	6 Years Pcnt	Rnk	10 Years Pcnt	Rnk
API Trust-Specl Markets (1992)	4.7	1	1.8	36	**	**	**	**	**	**	**	**
Boston Co. Inv-Asset Allocation A	2.8	8	3.4	28	10.7	20	11.9	12	-	-	-	-
Boston Co. Tr-Asset Manager's	2.6	9	3.5	26	9.0	28	-	-	-	-	-	-
Conn Mutual-Total Return	1.5	27	7.1	10	14.1	9	13.7	3	14.4	2	-	-
Crabbe Huson Asset Allocation	2.6	10	7.9	7	16.8	4	12.3	8	-	-	-	-
Dean Witter Managed Assets	0.8	34	5.2	17	8.6	30	10.5	21	-	-	-	-
Dean Witter Strategist Fund	1.7	23	3.2	29	9.7	26	11.3	16	-	-	-	-
Elfun Diversified Fund	1.6	25	3.0	32	11.2	17	11.1	17	12.4	6	-	-
Fidelity Asset Manager	2.1	14	8.9	5	16.0	3	16.2	2	-	-	-	-
Fortis Advantage-Asset Alloc	2.5	11	3.8	24	10.6	23	11.3	15	12.4	5	-	-
IAA Trust Asset Allocation Fd	0.6	37	3.9	23	8.9	29	10.0	24	9.6	17	10.1	1
J. Hancock Asset Allocation (1988)	3.7	3	2.1	35	14.8	6	10.3	23	**	**	**	**
Kidder Peabody Asset Alloc B	2.5	13	3.5	27	-	-	-	-	-	-	-	-
MIMLIC Asset Allocation (1987)	3.4	4	3.0	31	11.3	16	12.3	9	12.7	4	**	**
Merriman Asset Allocation	3.2	5	9.2	4	12.3	14	8.1	29	-	-	-	-
MetLife-State St. Mgd Assets	3.9	2	10.7	3	18.6	2	11.0	19	-	-	-	-
NY Life Instl Multi-Asset Fund	1.5	28	4.2	21	10.6	21	-	-	-	-	-	-
North American Asset Alloc	1.8	20	3.1	30	-	-	-	-	-	-	-	-
Oppenheimer Asset Allocation	2.8	7	6.9	11	11.8	16	10.3	22	11.2	12	-	-
Overland Express Asset Alloc	1.9	18	6.0	14	14.9	5	12.6	6	11.5	9	-	-
PaineWebber Asset Allocation B	1.2	31	2.2	34	6.7	32	8.5	27	8.7	18	-	-
Pasadena Balanced Return Fund	2.5	12	-2.4	37	4.4	33	10.5	20	15.2	1	-	-
Premier Capital Value A	0.5	38	11.3	2	1.9	34	4.1	32	7.4	20	-	-
Princor Managed Fund	1.4	29	4.2	20	9.7	25	13.2	4	10.9	13	-	-
Prudential Flexi-Conserv A	1.8	22	7.9	8	14.7	7	12.1	10	-	-	-	-
Prudential Flexi-Conserv B	1.8	21	7.5	9	13.7	10	12.0	11	11.4	10	-	-
Prudential Flexi-Strategy A	2.1	15	4.9	18	10.5	22	11.9	13	-	-	-	-
Prudential Flexi-Stragegy B	2.0	16	4.6	19	9.6	27	11.0	18	11.3	11	-	-
Quest for Value Opportunity	2.0	17	3.6	26	13.2	13	18.3	1	-	-	-	-
Seafirst Asset Allocation	1.6	26	5.6	16	8.1	31	9.8	25	11.9	7	-	-
Shearson Eq-Strategic Invest B	0.8	35	6.8	12	11.1	18	11.6	14	12.9	3	-	-
Stagecoach Asset Allocation	1.3	30	6.5	13	13.6	11	12.4	7	11.8	8	-	-
Stralem Fund	0.8	33	4.1	22	10.9	19	9.0	26	10.0	15	8.0	2
SunAmerica Total Return	1.8	19	8.4	6	13.3	12	7.3	30	9.8	16	-	-
Valley Forge Fund	3.0	6	14.9	1	18.9	1	8.2	28	8.3	19	8.0	3
Vanguard Asset Allocation	1.7	24	5.9	16	14.2	8	12.8	5	-	-	-	-
Westwood Equity Fund	0.7	36	2.9	33	10.2	24	7.1	31	10.7	14	-	-
Zweig Series Tr-Mgd Assets A	0.9	32	-	-	-	-	-	-	-	-	-	-
Totals and Averages	2.0	38	5.4	37	11.6	34	11.0	32	11.2	20	8.7	3

Source: CDA/Wiesenberger

tioned previously are less aggressively managed than many because they invest within a fixed percentage range of multiple assets. The newer funds, however, tend to be more aggressive. They switch among stocks, bonds, and cash based on the latest outlook for the financial markets. They rebalance more frequently based on their forecasts of how, for instance, stocks will outperform one-year T-bill rates and bonds.

These actively managed or "tactical-asset-allocation" portfolios change the investment mix based on the interaction between the outlook for the economy and the expected rate of return for each of the asset classes. Fidelity Investments' Asset Manager Fund, for example, uses a valuation model to spot opportunities in the equity markets. Vanguard's Asset Allocation Fund uses a dividend discount model to compare the expected rate of return on stocks with the return on one-year T-bills to find the right mix.

The goal of tactical funds is growth, but with lower risk than that of a fund investing only in stocks or bonds. Each fund calculates expected rates of return and economic projections differently. In essence, however, all funds seek to acquire the mix of assets with the highest expected rate of return at the lowest level of price volatility or standard deviation. Mixes may be rebalanced monthly, quarterly, or semiannually, depending on the manager's forecasts and the financial news. If high inflation and rising interest rates are expected, the portfolio would be heavily weighted in cash and inflation hedges such as gold or real estate. During periods of declining interest rates, the bond portion would increase. Assets would be shifted into stocks when lower interest rates begin to spur economic growth.

One such fund, the Paine Webber Asset Allocation Fund, seeks high total return with low volatility by investing in a combination of stocks, bonds, and money-market instruments. The fund has the flexibility to be 100 percent invested in any of these assets. The fund manager compares expected rates of return on these securities with the S&P 500 and the presumed return on ten-year Treasury bonds and three-month T-bills. The fund manager then creates a blend with the best risk-adjusted rate of return. The combination then is adjusted monthly.

The MIMLIC Asset Allocation Fund takes a different approach to tactile asset allocation. The fund manager buys growth stocks, bonds, and cash. He moves among the assets incrementally. He will switch no more than 5 percent in any quarter. He invests in assets with the best expected rates of return.

Paul Merriman, president of Paul Merriman & Associates and publisher of the *Fund Exchange,* Seattle Washington, launched a unique family of mutual funds a few years ago. He uses market timing strategies based on price and economic trends to switch between stocks, bonds, or cash in each fund depending on a fund's investment objective.

The four funds in the Merriman Investment Trust included a timed government bond fund, blue-chip stock fund, growth stock fund and asset allocation fund. The funds are no-load, have a 1 to 1.5 percent management fee and require a $1,000 initial investment.

Merriman says that his funds differ from the others because he uses market timing strategies to move in and out of the financial markets. Though financial research has revealed that over the long term of 5 to 60 years market timing doesn't work, Merriman defends his switch strategy. He says that since 1983 he's been in stocks and bonds about 85 percent of the time and has shown a profit. In bad years when the stock and bond markets have dropped he's broken even.

Merriman says he uses several market timing systems to buy and sell in each fund. He believes investors will get more downside protection, if several systems are used. In addition, he will invest in other mutual funds with long-term track records like 20th Century, Nicholas, Janus, Columbia Growth, and SAFECO.

There are passively managed balanced funds which may also be considered asset allocation funds. The funds use a fixed percentage range to invest in multiple-asset classes that include domestic and foreign securities, inflation hedges such as gold and real estate, stocks and cash.

Though they may shift some assets, funds that hold more assets tend to protect themselves by making sure a certain percentage always is invested in cash and inflation hedges.

The BB&K Diverse Fund is one fund that takes a more aggressive approach to multiple-asset management. The fund seeks above-average total return with below-average risk by investing in five classes of securities: stocks, bonds, foreign securities, real estate securities, and cash. The fund will hold at least 5 percent and no more than 50 percent of its assets in each class of securities. Cash holdings range from 0 to 25 percent, and the fund will not invest more than 25 percent of its assets in any one real estate–related industry. The advisor performs an asset-allocation review at least semiannually.

BB&K asset-allocation decisions are based on the expected rates of return of both individual securities and classes of securities. Probably outcomes in each class will be reviewed to decide the best mix. The classes of securities then are ranked by expected rate of return, yield, investor sentiment, and historic volatility. A simulation study is conducted to see how the chosen mix performs under conditions of high inflation or economic depression. If the real returns, or return less inflation, of the portfolio are zero or positive, the fund management assumes its portfolio could weather any economic storm, at least over a four-year period.

The more passive multiple-asset funds mentioned previously have fixed investment–percentage ranges.

USAA Cornerstone seeks to preserve the purchasing power of shareholders' capital and attain positive real return. To accomplish this, the fund invests approximately 18 to 20 percent of its assets in each of the following categories: gold, foreign stocks, real estate stocks, U.S. government securities, and undervalued U.S. stocks.

Permanent Portfolio seeks to preserve and increase purchasing power by using an investment model consisting of 20 percent of assets in gold, 5 percent in silver, 10 percent in Swiss franc assets, 15 percent in U.S. and foreign stocks, and 35 percent in U.S. T-bills and other dollar assets.

Blanchard Strategic Growth takes a more aggressive stance to achieving long-term capital growth. The fund invests in U.S. stocks, foreign stocks, precious-metals stocks, bullion, and fixed-income securities. The fund will change the mix quarterly based on economic and investment conditions.

DO SOME UNDERCOVER WORK

If you are inclined to invest in an all-in-one fund, you should ask the following questions before you invest:

- How flexible is the fund? Does it use market timing and turn the portfolio over more than 100 percent a year? The greater the flexibility, the greater the potential for larger gains or larger losses. Do you want an asset-allocation growth fund or are you looking for safety?
- Most of these asset-allocation funds are new; they have no track record. Watch to see how well they perform over at least one up market and one down market. Check the record of existing funds if the allocation funds is part of a fund family. Also check the experience of the people responsible for making the asset-allocation decisions. How many years of experience do they have managing money both here and overseas? If there is a team of portfolio managers, ask about their backgrounds and what kind of input they have in reaching asset-allocation decisions. How are they compensated? If each manager is rewarded for performance, infighting could

154

detract from the managers' ability to make the proper allocation decisions.

- Does the fund practice rebalancing? Does its management take profits in winning assets and dollar cost average into investments that have declined? Rebalancing is a more conservative way to invest.
- If fund managers are making investment decisions based on historical price and performance correlations, what time periods are they using? The shorter the time period, the more aggressively the manager is looking for trends that he or she hopes will continue. A longer time period, such as ten years or more, indicates a less-aggressive fund manager.
- Check the number of asset classes open for investment. Funds that can invest in overseas stocks and bonds, precious metals, and real estate offer you more diversification. If a fund uses an index portfolio, check to see if the index is capitalization weighted. If it is, the fund manager must match the market value of the stocks in the index proportionately in order to receive the same return. The fund manager may have to trade more to keep the portfolio in balance. Or he or she may have to invest in stock index futures and option contracts. Both these tactics rack up transaction or brokerage commissions.
- Pick a fund with a low fee structure. Note any front-end load or sales charges, management fees, 12b-1 or sales-distributions fees and back-end deferred sales changes. By law, mutual funds are required to list all charges in the beginning of each prospectus, along with how much you would earn, less the fee, over five- and ten-year periods.

KEEP ABREAST OF YOUR BUDGET
AND INVESTMENTS

Whether you invested in one of the all-weather mutual funds or set up your own investment mix, check your portfolio's performance at least quarterly. If the returns continually lag behind those of the benchmarks, consider changing funds, stocks, or your mix. If your financial status changes, you should consider reducing the risk of your portfolio. If you have experienced a recent cash drain—such as buying a car or making a major repair—or you can foresee this type of drain, preservation of principal suddenly is more important to you than it was before. You do not want to risk additional losses on your life savings. You may feel that you cannot afford so much risk as you thought you could. If this is the case, it might be better to move money out of stocks and into bonds and cash until your situation improves.

PART
3

Asset-Allocation Strategies

CHAPTER 8

Dollar Cost Averaging

No one knows what the future might bring. Kansas City Royals ace relief pitcher Dan Quisenberry had quite an unusual insight. After striking out the last batter in the bottom of the ninth inning and securing a victory for his team, he said, "I've seen the future and it looks like the present, only it's longer."

Like a championship ball team, investors need a winning investment coach: a coach who can protect a lead, who knows whether you are going to win or lose in the future. To procure this kind of assistance, safety-conscious investors should consider using dollar cost averaging as a way to invest in stocks and bonds.

IT'S NOT SCINTILLATING

Dollar cost averaging (DCA) entails making periodic payments of a fixed amount, such as $100 a month, over a time span of at least ten years to buy individual securities or mutual funds. DCA works best in retirement savings plans: It forces you to make a disciplined, long-term commitment to an investment that grows tax-deferred until you take distributions at retirement. When you buy in a disciplined manner, you buy more shares at a lower price when prices are falling. On the upside, you also accumulate shares at lower prices if the market keeps rising. Over the long term, your periodic purchases will result in an average cost that will be lower than the market price.

DCA is a safe way for the average person to invest for it eliminates market timing decisions. Most investors tend to buy at market peaks when mutual funds or stocks are receiving a great deal of media attention; unfortunately, these are the points at which the market usually plunges. Or, in a falling market, investors typically buy, hold, pray and eventually panic and sell at the worst possible times, as the market bottoms out before a rebound.

Dollar cost averaging eliminates the guesswork. You always will be fully invested to catch the turns in the market. This hypothetical example shows you how it works.

- In a declining market, if you made a series of $400 investments, your breakdown might look like this:

Investment	Share Price	Shares Bought
$ 400	$16	25
400	10	40
400	8	50
400	8	50
400	5	80
$2,000	$47	245

As you can see, the price of the shares dropped from $16 to $5. Your average share cost was $8.16

160

or $2,000 divided by 245. Your average share price was $9.40 or $47 divided by 5. As a result, you would realize a profit if the market rebounded above the $9.40 level of your average share price.
• When the market moves up, your DCA program might look like this:

Investment	Share Price	Shares Bought
$ 400	$ 5	80
400	8	50
400	10	40
400	10	40
400	16	25
$2,000	$49	235

As you can see from this example designed by the Vanguard Group of Funds, your average share cost was $8.15 or $2,000 divided by 235. Your average share price was $9.80 or $49 divided by 5. By averaging on the upside, you can see that you kept your average share and cost prices far below the high of $16 per share.

Suppose you decide to sell your shares. Because there is no sure thing with dollar cost averaging, you still must wait for a favorable time to sell. Assuming there have been no dividend or capital-gains distributions, for example, you have made $4,000 at an average share price of $9.60 and at an average cost of $8.33. You now own 480 shares. What if the price shoots up to $20 per share? It may take a year for that to happen, but once it does, you have made a sizable profit. If the money is in a retirement savings plan, keep it invested for the long term. If you cost-averaged into a stock that was not part of a retirement plan, you could sell 480 shares at $20 and collect $9,600, a tidy profit.

A PROVEN COMMODITY

In the real world, over the past 15 years—as an example using the Vanguard Index 500 fund, an equity fund that tracks the market averages—using the DCA strategy has been successful. From July 1976 through June 1992, a $100-a-month DCA program resulted in an average cost per share of $22.47. The market price of the fund stood at $38.58 by the end of June and the $18,000 total investment was worth $62,651.

If you had been in a dollar-cost-averaging program during the October 1987 stock-market plunge, you would have been able to buy more shares at a lower price in the Vanguard Index Fund and reap the ensuing gains when the market rebounded (see Table 8.1). Your $100 investment would have bought you extra shares when the fund's net asset value declined from $32.31. In October of 1987, you could have bought shares for $25.29; in November, for $23.22. In succeeding months, you would have accumulated shares at between $5 to $7 less than the fund's high price for the year, which was $33.75. Through July of 1988, the value of your periodic payments would have grown 12 percent in ten months.

A FEW STRINGS

Dollar cost averaging is one of the safest ways to play the stock market, but the method does have its pitfalls. You cannot absolutely guarantee that the average cost will be lower than the market value when you redeem. You also must be careful not to invest too large a sum at once, otherwise your losses could mount up quickly.

Bull markets historically last longer than bear markets, so in many cases investors may not be able to buy enough low-cost shares during down cycles to make DCA as profitable as investing a lump sum in a bull market. For investors to accumulate enough money in a

Table 8.1   Dollar Cost Averaging with Vanguard Index 500

Year	Month	Return	Contribution	Account Balance
	July	−1.5282	100	98.47
	August	−1.4022	100	195.89
	September	.0074	100	295.71
	October	−4.1572	100	379.28
	November	3.4700	100	495.89
	December	.5335	100	599.07
1978	January	−5.9954	100	657.16
	February	−1.7171	100	744.16
	March	2.5762	100	865.91
	April	8.5316	100	1,048.31
	May	1.2850	100	1,163.07
	June	−1.5880	100	1,243.26
	July	5.6705	100	1,419.43
	August	3.4083	100	1,571.22
	September	−.5554	100	1,661.94
	October	−8.9031	100	1,605.07
	November	2.5801	100	1,749.06
	December	1.6742	100	1,880.02
1979	January	4.1190	100	2,061.58
	February	−2.8571	100	2,099.82
	March	5.7258	100	2,325.78
	April	.3605	100	2,434.52
	May	−1.6523	100	2,492.64
	June	4.0191	100	2,698.84
	July	1.1356	100	2,828.61
	August	6.1053	100	3,107.41
	September	.1984	100	3,213.77
	October	−6.5333	100	3,097.27
	November	5.1355	100	3,361.47
	December	1.7622	100	3,522.46
1980	January	5.9426	100	3,837.73
	February	.3868	100	3,952.96
	March	−9.8123	100	3,655.28
	April	4.3228	100	3,917.61
	May	5.5249	100	4,239.58
	June	2.7982	100	4,461.01
	July	6.6238	100	4,863.12
	August	1.2666	100	5,025.98
	September	2.6802	100	5,263.37
	October	1.9906	100	5,470.13
	November	10.9644	100	6,180.66
	December	−3.1429	100	6,083.46
1981	January	−4.4283	100	5,909.64
	February	2.1114	100	6,136.53
	March	3.7440	100	6,470.02
	April	−2.1812	100	6,426.72
	May	.6289	100	6.567.78
	June	−.8523	100	6,610.93
	July	.0000	100	6,710.93
	August	−5.4430	100	6.440.22
	September	−5.0214	100	6,211.81
	October	5.2185	100	6,641.19
	November	4.4017	100	7,037.91
	December	−2.7549	100	6,941.27
1982	January	−1.4820	100	6,936.92
	February	−5.1014	100	6,677.94
	March	−.6927	100	6,730.99
	April	4.1462	100	7,114.21
	May	−2.8340	100	7,009.78
	June	−1.6034	100	6,995.76
	July	−2.2159	100	6,938.53
	August	12.4269	100	7,913.20
	September	1.0135	100	8,094.41

Continued

Table 8.1 Continued

Year	Month	Return	Contribution	Account Balance
	October	11.1328	100	9,106.68
	November	4.2765	100	9,600.41
	December	1.6819	100	9,863.56
1983	January	3.4169	100	10,304.00
	February	2.4780	100	10,661.81
	March	3.5014	100	11,138.63
	April	7.5996	100	12,092.72
	May	−.8768	100	12,085.81
	June	3.7475	100	12,642.48
	July	−3.2489	100	12,328.49
	August	1.8272	100	12,655.58
	September	1.2513	100	12,815.19
	October	−1.4010	100	12,832.85
	November	2.2538	100	13,224.33
	December	−.6355	100	13,239.65
1984	January	−.5076	100	13,271.94
	February	−3.3163	100	12,928.49
	March	1.6314	100	13,241.03
	April	.7338	100	13,438.93
	May	−5.4110	100	12,806.34
	June	2.2024	100	13,190.59
	July	−1.4674	100	13,095.56
	August	11.1969	100	14,673.05
	September	.0000	100	14,773.05
	October	.2503	100	14,910.26
	November	−.9985	100	14,860.40
	December	2.5953	100	15,348.67
1985	January	7.5820	100	16,619.88
	February	1.3810	100	16,950.89
	March	.0052	100	17,051.78
	April	−.2842	100	17,103.03
	May	6.0333	100	18,240.94
	June	1.4333	100	18,603.82
	July	−.2226	100	18,662.19
	August	−.6693	100	18,636.61
	September	−3.1447	100	18,147.40
	October	4.3986	100	19,049.67
	November	6.9444	100	20,479.50
	December	4.6738	100	21,541.34
1986	January	.4350	100	21,735.48
	February	7.5790	100	23,490.40
	March	5.4750	100	24,881.97
	April	−1.3451	100	24,645.94
	May	5.4538	100	26,095.53
	June	1.6858	100	26,631.90
	July	−5.7425	100	25,196.82
	August	7.4505	100	27,181.56
	September	−8.3062	100	25,015.50
	October	5.6327	100	26,530.16
	November	2.5535	100	27,310.18
	December	−2.6413	100	26,686.18
1987	January	13.2674	100	30,340.02
	February	3.9651	100	31,647.00
	March	2.8950	100	32,666.08
	April	−1.0263	100	32,429.80
	May	1.0370	100	32,867.13
	June	5.0213	100	34,622.51
	July	4.9148	100	36,429.05
	August	3.8413	100	37,932.24
	September	−2.2855	100	37,163.02
	October	−21.7270	100	29,166.88
	November	−8.1851	100	28,871.36
	December	7.5507	100	29,007.88

Continued

Table 8.1 Continued

Year	Month	Return	Contribution	Account Balance
1988	January	4.1746	100	30,323.02
	February	4.5900	100	31,819.44
	March	−3.0411	100	30,948.74
	April	1.0129	100	31,363.23
	May	.8099	100	31,718.05
	June	4.5555	100	33,267.52
	July	−.3683	100	33,244.63
	August	−3.4011	100	32,210.54
	September	4.2555	100	33,685.52
	October	2.7347	100	34,709.45
	November	−1.4029	100	34,321.11
	December	1.6635	100	34,993.71
1989	January	7.3216	100	37,663.13
	February	−2.4683	100	36,631.02
	March	2.2599	100	37,765.62
	April	5.1844	100	39,828.73
	May	4.0357	100	41,540.13
	June	−.5860	100	41,396.12
	July	9.0061	100	45,233.30
	August	1.8590	100	46,176.05
	September	−.4046	100	46,088.62
	October	−2.3392	100	45,108.37
	November	2.0359	100	46,128.76
	December	2.3758	100	47,327.07
1990	January	−6.7182	100	44,240.82
	February	1.2747	100	44,906.03
	March	2.6073	100	46,179.48
	April	−2.5015	100	45,121.80
	May	9.6927	100	49,605.01
	June	−.6888	100	49,362.64
	July	−.3215	100	49,303.62
	August	−9.0323	100	44,941.34
	September	−4.8904	100	42,838.63
	October	−.4093	100	42,762.89
	November	6.4384	100	45,622.57
	December	2.7154	100	46,964.12
1991	January	4.3214	100	49,097.95
	February	7.1494	100	52,715.31
	March	2.4053	100	54,085.67
	April	.1971	100	54,292.47
	May	4.2721	100	56,716.18
	June	−4.5592	100	54,225.81
	July	4.6267	100	56,839.30
	August	2.3332	100	58,267.81
	September	−1.6684	100	57,394.00
	October	1.3276	100	58,257.29
	November	−4.0107	100	56,016.76
	December	11.4134	100	62,521.59
1992	January	−1.8820	100	61,443.05
	February	1.2442	100	62,308.77
	March	−1.9257	100	61,206.96
	April	2.9142	100	63,093.57
	May	.4847	100	63,499.87
	June	−1.4915	100	62,651.28

165

dollar-cost-averaging program for gains to become substantial profits usually takes from five to ten years. Over the short term, the performance of dollar cost averaging will lag behind other investing methods. And, although aggressive-stock funds or gold funds are the best vehicles for DCA because they are volatile and DCA capitalizes on price fluctuation, the danger always exists that the fund will not rebound sufficiently.

You must be patient to succeed at dollar cost averaging. You may experience years during which the market is flat and you are accumulating shares at about the same price. A study conducted by Sheldon Jacobs of the *No Load Investor* newsletter found that during the flat market years of 1971 through 1976, the difference between the average share price at the beginning and at the end was only 21 cents. DCA performed poorly, he concluded, because only a small portion of money was invested at the beginning of the period. Most of the money was invested at times when prices were appreciating.

You also may experience a period when the financial markets move like a seesaw, as was the case from 1965 through 1970. A jerky market means few time periods when you can buy shares at a price low enough for regular buying to pay off.

At other times, DCA will not fare so well as a lump-sum. Let's look at the period before the stock market crash in 1987. Figure 8.1 shows how the strategy worked against a lump sum that was divided 50-50 between stocks and bonds. During the down market from January 1, 1973 through December 31, 1974, DCA kept its value, while a lump-sum $10,000 investment lost $1,700. During the trendless market from February 1, 1977, through January 31, 1979, both the lump-sum and the DCA programs held their initial values. In the up market from January 1, 1985, through December 31, 1986, however, DCA gains lagged behind those of a buy-and-hold investment.

Figure 8.1   **Dollar Cost Averaging versus Buy and Hold**

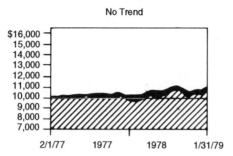

No Trend

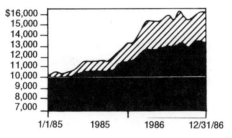

Up

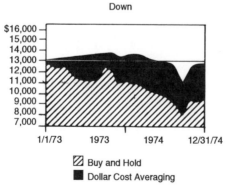

Down

◫ Buy and Hold
■ Dollar Cost Averaging

Source: Colonial Investment Services, Inc.

167

The pattern holds true today. DCA is a safe way to invest. You will underperform a lump sum in a bull market. But when stocks plunged in October of 1987, investors that used DCA accumulated fund shares at an attractive price. They assumed less risk because they bought at lower prices when the stock market tumbled and benefited when the market rebounded.

The S&P 500 grew at an annual rate of 14.21 percent in the five years ensuing the stock market crash of 1987. You just about double your money with a lump-sum investment.

But who had the guts to stick in a lump sum in the market after the crash? Not many. For those who wanted to play it safe and still keep a hand in the market, DCA did fine. A $100-a-month investment grew to about $8,684.

DCA is not a perfect way to invest, but in a well thought-out diversified investment plan, it is a safe way to invest for long-term horizons of ten years or more.

CHAPTER 9

Formula Investing

Let's face it, if you take big risks you will either win big or lose big. As Will Rogers once said, "Don't gamble. Take all your savings and buy some good stock and hold it til it goes up, then sell it. If it don't go up, don't buy it."

Like dollar cost averaging, formula-investment strategies enable you to take profits, buy more shares when prices decline and reduce risk. Using predetermined sell points to rebalance your portfolio works well when you allocate assets. This diversified investment mix will prevent you from losing your shirt, as many investors do, when experiencing extreme stock- and bond-market volatility.

Investors who bought and held stocks or bonds over the past ten years, despite some scary corrections, realized sizable gains. You would have quadrupled (stocks) or more than doubled (bonds) your money. The October 1987 stock-market crash, however, still is fresh in people's minds. That experience, coupled with today's uncertain economic environment, dictates considering more than just a buy-and-hold investment scheme.

YOU CANNOT BEAT A BULL MARKET

You cannot beat a buy-and-hold strategy in a bull market. Ideally, you would be fully invested from day one and would receive the benefits of compounding stock prices and reinvestment of dividends and capital gains. Over the past ten years, the S&P 500 have grown at an annual rate of 16 percent. At that rate, money doubles every four and one-half years. If you look at a chart of the S&P 500, you will see the stock lines rising at almost a 45-degree angle. With that kind of upswing, even random switching between stocks and money funds makes you money. There are no stupid investors in a bull market.

Several funds have racked up even bigger gains than that over the past ten years. The Fidelity Magellan Fund grew at an annual rate of 28.9 percent over the decade ending in July of 1988. Magellan's performance has slowed down. However, for ten years ending in March of 1993, the fund grew at an annual rate of 17.4 percent, compared to the 14.4 percent annual return on the market.

Of course, who knew ten years ago that we would experience one of the greatest bull markets in history? How many investors have the intestinal fortitude to hold on to sizable lump-sum investments as they lose money? The Magellan Fund, for instance, lost 21 percent in October of 1978, 10 percent in October of 1979 and 33 percent in October and November of 1987.

Many investment advisors say that we have seen the last gasps of the great bull market. You cannot invest on past performance. The 1980s may become known in the future as the great buy-and-hold decade, but the 1990s may be called the decade of risk-controlled investing.

INVESTING FOR UNCERTAIN TIMES

Dollar cost averaging has been the traditional way to invest to reduce uncertainty. Dollar cost averaging, however, is not without problems, for it calls for some type of market-timing sell decisions, particularly for those who are about to receive distributions from retirement plans.

RULES FOR TIMING BUYING AND SELLING

Constant-dollar and constant-ratio investment strategies are variations on dollar cost averaging that help control risk and eliminate market-timing sell decisions. Formula investing is based on the simple idea that you take predetermined levels of profits in your aggressive investments and salt away the money in conservative investments such as money funds or bond funds. This switching enables you to avoid market-timing decisions. When your aggressive investments decline to a specified level, you switch money from your conservative portfolio into your aggressive portfolio. This way, you take profits and dollar-cost-average as prices decline. On the upside, you realize profits and park them in a safe place.

CONSTANT-DOLLAR PLAN

The constant-dollar value plan is one tactic that employs the principles of dollar cost averaging and risk aversion to build wealth. Under this plan, the dollar value of your aggressive investments will remain constant after passing through a predetermined time period. Money then would be channeled into a bond fund or from the bond fund into a stock fund to maintain the constant-dollar investment strategy. Bond or money funds are appropriate counterbalances because they have low correlations to equities. As a result, during recessionary periods when stocks perform poorly, gains in bonds will offset losses in the equity markets as interest rates decline. For investors who do not want the volatility associated with bonds, money funds may be the safest parking place.

IT'S EASY TO DO

Here is how the constant dollar strategy would work using an aggressive-growth stock fund and a bond or money fund. Table 9.1 shows you how the investment performed during the initial stages of the bull market that started in 1982 and ended in 1990. You decided to keep a constant-dollar amount of $10,000 in your aggressive portfolio and are willing to accept a 20-percent gain or loss in that portfolio every six months. After six months, if the value of your stock fund has grown to $12,000, you would take out $2,000 and move it into your bond or money fund. Conversely, if the value of your stock fund has dropped to $8,000 after six months, you would switch $2,000 out of bonds and into stocks to maintain the constant-dollar value of $10,000. You use the bond fund or money fund as a parking place—the only reason to change its value is to move money in and out of stocks.

Table 9.1 shows how the trades are made. You invested $10,000 in both a stock and bond fund and are willing to take out $2,000 in profits, or 20 percent, when the value of your stock fund grows to $12,000 after six months. You also are willing to take $2,000 or more out of your bond fund when the value of your stock fund declines to $8,000 or less. Your trades might look like this: In the second half of 1982 you earned $2,700 in your stock fund. You rebalance your stock fund back to $10,000 and put the profits in your bond fund. In the second half of 1983, however, the market value of your stock fund declined $3,000, so you took money out of your bond fund and rebalanced the equity side to $10,000. Over the next 18 months, the value of the stock fund fluctuates within your trading limits and by the middle of 1985 the fund is worth $11,800. But by

Table 9.1 Stock- and Bond-Fund Trades

Date	Stock-Fund $	Bond-Fund $	Total-Value $
6/31/82	$10,000	$10,000	$20,000
7/82 to 12/82 reb.	12,700 10,000	12,480 15,100	25,100 25,100
1/83 to 6/83	11,000	16,610	27,610
7/83 to 12/83 reb.	8,000 10,000	16,859 14,859	24,859 24,859
1/84 to 6/84	9,150	13,859	23,009
7/84 to 12/84	10,980	16,076	27,056
1/85 to 6/85	11,800	17,683	29,483
7/85 to 12/85 reb.	13,900 10,000	19,100 23,000	33,024 33,024

year-end 1985, the fund has grown to $13,900 and the total value is $33,024.

Over the long term a constant dollar investment tactic will under perform DCA. You take profits and dollar cost average with constant dollar investing. As a result, you take money out of stocks in a bull market. By contrast, you are always fully invested in stocks when you DCA. For example: If you maintain a constant dollar amount of $10,000 in the S&P 500 every year by rebalancing, your money grew to $49,540 over the past 15 years. By contrast, DCA gain over $60,000 with a $100 a month investment over the same time.

MATCHING YOUR COMFORT LEVEL

The trick with the constant-dollar plan is to match your risk tolerance with the appropriate evaluation period. If you take profits too quickly, you could end up with too many trades and miss major market moves on the upside. In addition, if the investments are not part of a retirement savings plan, you also may pay too much capital-gains tax. It is best to check your aggressive portfolio semiannually to maintain a constant-dollar amount in equities. A 15 to 20 percent gain or loss is an appropriate benchmark. At these levels, you are banking profits and buying on the low side.

BANKING PROFITS

You can't beat a long-term buy-and-hold investment, even when the stock market tumbles. Figure 9.1 shows you how several easy to use investment tactics worked for ten years that included the stock market crash of 1987, when the average equity fund lost 20 percent in the last three months of the year.

Figure 9.1 **Alternative Investment Strategies Over the Ten Years Ending 7/31/88**

Unless otherwise indicated, portfolios are equally weighted at $10,000 each in Salomon Bros. Corporate Bond Index and Fidelity Magellan Fund.

Strategy	Dollar Value	Annual Return
Constant Dollar Readjusted Every Six Months or 20% Change	$ 81,886	15.1%
Buy & Hold	$153,325	22.6%
Buy & Hold Standard & Poor's 500 Index ($20,000)	$ 85,002	15.6%
Buy & Hold Salomon Bros. Corp. Bond Index ($20,000)	$ 53,111	10.3%
Buy & Hold Fidelity Magellan Fund ($20,000)	$253,540	28.9%
Dollar Cost Averaging	$ 61,048	—
Dollar Cost Averaging Fidelity Magellan Fund	$ 83,655	—

Source: Alan Lavine Financial Planning

Buying and holding Fidelity Magellan fund or the S&P 500 outperformed the formula investment strategies. Magellan gained a whopping 28.9 percent annual for ten years ending in 7/31/88. By contrast the S&P 500 gained 15.6 percent. Even a lump sum investment in Magellan and bonds grew at an annual rate of 22.6 percent.

No conservative tactic can top that performance. And we are unlikely to see such stellar returns in the 1990s. Most experts will be lucky if the average stock fund grows at an annual rate of 10 percent over the next ten years.

NO SURE-FIRE WINNERS

Formula investing is not a get-rich-quick scheme. It must be used over several business cycles. The constant-dollar tactic earns most in a market with a steep drop, in which you average down, followed by a resurgent bull. In a rising market, such as we recently have experienced, the constant-dollar plan does well against a dollar-cost averaging program split between stocks and bonds, but fails to beat a buy-and-hold. In a sideways market, your performance might mimic that of a buy-and-hold strategy, but your after-tax return would be lower if you were forced to do some switching.

A formula plan can be inflexible: If market conditions change, the predetermined sell points may not work. In the slow-growth economy expected in 1989, for example, investors may prefer to shorten their holding period and sell points to maximize their positions.

You also must choose the right type of aggressive-stock fund to make formula investing work. Look for low- or no-load aggressive-stock funds that show strong rebounds from their lows. Total return funds, or mutual funds that adjust their cash, stock, and bond mixes, may be inappropriate. Aggressive funds that remain fully invested in the stock market allow you to maximize your returns and place profits into cash or bonds. Always look at the investment strategy of an equity fund before you invest.

CONSTANT-RATIO INVESTING

The constant-ratio investment plan is another way to buy more shares when prices decline. By maintaining a constant ratio of stocks to bonds or cash over a period of time, you are rebalancing your portfolio by taking profits on the upside and dollar cost averaging on the downside when the investment declines.

If you keep one-third of your investment in a growth-stock fund and two-thirds in a money or bond fund, that combination would translate into a ratio of 50 percent—one-third divided by two-thirds equals .50. Every six months you would check the ratio of stocks to bonds or cash and bring it back to 50 percent, if necessary. You would rebalance in a way similar to the method depicted in Figure 9.2.

A PRACTICUM

If you started with $20,000—$6,600 in a growth fund and $13,400 in a money fund that earned 3.5 percent semiannually—and the growth fund lost 5.6 percent over six months, the new value of your portfolio would be $6,244 in stocks and $13,869 in cash, a total of $20,113. The ratio of stocks to bonds has dropped to 45 percent, so you must readjust it. You shift your money to position $7,626 (or one-third of the total value) into stocks and the remaining two-thirds, or $13,947, into cash.

PROFIT-TAKING PLUS DOLLAR COST AVERAGING

The constant-ratio methodology combines the best of both worlds: You have a predetermined sell point and

Figure 9.2   **Formula Investing Strategies Over the Ten Years Ending 6/30/88**

Strategy	Annual Return	Ending Value of $20,000 Portfolio
1/3 Fidelity Magellan, 2/3 cash @7%	12.6%	$65,357
1/3 Fidelity Magellan, 2/3 Salomon Bros. Corp. Bond Index	14.8%	$79,184
Dollar Cost Averaging Fidelity Magellan ($20,000 over 10 years monthly)	NA	$83,655
Buy and Hold $20,000 Standard and Poor's 500	15.6%	$85,002
Buy and Hold $20,000 Salomon Bros. Corporate Bonds	10.3%	$53,111

Source: Alan Lavine Financial Planning

you dollar cost average as prices fall. Over the past ten years, based on our studies, this strategy would have earned a return about half way between the buy-and-hold return on the S&P 500 and that of the Salomon Brothers Corporate Bond Average. The result assumes you kept a constant ratio of 1 or a 50/50 stock bond split.

Say you put $5,000 in a stock fund that tracked the S&P 500 and $5,000 in a bond fund that moved in tandem with the bond market average and you rebalance the portfolio every year: Your investment grew to $53,145 over the past ten years at an annual average rate of 11.8 percent.

Historically, you earn about 80 percent of the return on the stock market with about 50 percent less downside risk with a 50/50 or 60/40 stock and bond investment mix that's rebalanced yearly.

If you want to play it safe, stick with a constant ratio investment mix. More aggressive investors can keep more of their portfolio in a stock fund. Someone age 35, for example, could put 65 percent in a stock fund and 35 percent in a bond fund.

REBALANCING YOUR DIVERSIFIED PORTFOLIO

The rebalancing strategy goes one step further than the other formula plans. When you rebalance, you maintain the same constant percentage mix in your diversified portfolio. The size and allocation of the percentage portions can be tailored to your specific situation. To cut your risk in the stock and bond markets, you could divide your portfolio into fifths, with 20 percent each in stocks, gold, international stocks, U.S. corporate bonds and money funds. Every year, you must check the total value of your portfolio and place 20 percent of that total into each of your investment segments. This rebalancing usually dictates some switching around and some tax consequences if the money is not invested in a retirement savings plan. By rebalancing, though, you actualize your profits and dollar-cost-average with the investments that have faltered temporarily.

HOW IT WORKS

Let's look at how rebalancing a diversified portfolio works during two different ten-year periods from 1978 through 1988 and for ten years ending in 1993. Assume that at the end of 1978 you placed 20 percent of your investment, or $5,000, in the Vanguard Index 500 Fund (an equity fund that mimics the performance of the S&P 500), the United Services Gold Fund, the Scudder International Fund, the Fidelity Capital and Income Fund, and a money-market fund. At the end of the year, the total value of your portfolio rose by $7,389. Divided by five, you obtain $1,477.80, the sum that should be in each fund for the next 12 months. At the end of 1980, you check your total again. The portfolio grew to $9,659—divided by five, that leaves $1,942 in each fund.

Rebalancing works well for several reasons. Investments such as those listed previously tend to move in contrary directions. If one does poorly, another may produce offsetting gains. Because you are dollar-cost-averaging, you buy low and sell high when you rebalance. Rebalancing eliminates market-timing decisions.

Let's see how the timing works with the funds we just mentioned. In 1981—a bad year for stocks because interest rates were at double-digit levels—Vanguard Index 500 lost 5.2 percent, the United Services Gold Fund dropped 27.9 percent and the Scudder International Fund 2.6 percent. Only the money fund, which paid 17.3 percent interest, survived the interest-rate debacle. The $9,659 you ended 1980 with falls to $9,433 by the end of the year. You have lost 2.34 percent on your investment, or $226. With all of your money in stocks, you would have lost $502. With all of your money in gold, you would have lost $2,695.

Your $9,433 at the end of 1981 ($1,887 for each investment sector) would have surged in 1982, for that year inaugurated our record bull market. Stocks gained 21.3 percent and money funds yielded 12.8 percent; at the same time precious metals rebounded to a 72.5 percent return. As a result, your total portfolio grew to $12,298.

Don't be too impressed with these numbers. Past performance is no indication of future results; if that were the case, everyone capable of reading a newspaper would be rich. The portfolio we back-tested and rebalanced from year-end 1978 to year-end 1988 grew to $23,606, reflecting an annual average return of 16.7 percent. Unfortunately, no one knows where today's portfolios will be in ten years.

Rebalancing the same portfolio for ten years ending in 1993 achieved similar results. Investment conditions changed. The results show that you earned less in the most recent ten-year period compared to the period ending in 1988. But don't forget, the market earned less. What you got was a lower risk/return.

By keeping 20 percent in each fund annually the portfolio grew at an 8 percent annual rate. This is half the return for the same portfolio that gained 16.7 percent for ten years ending in 1978.

You earned less, but diversification worked. In 1990 the average growth fund lost over 5 percent and international stock funds dropped 11 percent.

How did our mix perform? We had a bad year. The Vanguard Index 500 lost 3.3 percent. The U.S. Gold Fund dropped 34.2 percent. Scudder International fund declined 8.9 percent, Fidelity Capital and Income lost 3.8 percent. Fortunately our money fund gained 8 percent. Since we had 20 percent in each asset we lost 8.4 percent in 1990.

Sometimes you have to take your lumps, even when you diversify. But look what happened in the following year. The markets rallied and our diversified portfolio gained a respectable 12.4 percent. Big winners were the Vanguard 500 Fund and the Fidelity Capital and Income Fund which both gained 30 percent.

At the time of this writing precious metals mutual funds are up 40 percent and international funds gained 13 percent. By contrast our markets are sluggish. The S&P is up just 2 percent year-to-date and bonds are up 5.5 percent. Small company growth stocks, on average, are down 1.5 percent.

As you can see the whole is always greater than the sum of its parts. If you have a diversified portfolio of mutual funds, you may have different winners and losers each year. But what's important is that you get the best overall return with the least amount of risk.

SAFETY IS THE KEY

The important point about rebalancing is the process: spreading your risks and realizing your profits without trying to guess the best time to buy or sell.

REBALANCE BASED ON YOUR RISK LEVEL

The 20-percent rebalancing tactic works well to reduce risk. This percentage breakdown may not be ideal for everyone, however. A couple approaching retirement should take less risk than a young professional couple with a combined income of more than $125,000 a year. Younger people can afford to seek growth and take more risk because they can buy and hold for a longer time as well as anticipate a longer period of generating (probably rising) income. The preretirement couple may want some growth, but they also need safety. They would be aghast to see the value of their portfolio drop 20 percent a few years before they retire.

This is why it is important to match investment risk with financial needs and risk tolerance. When you look at your risk level and income and growth requirements, you can set a better investment mix. Examine the following factors:

- How closely do investments move in tandem with each other? You want a mix where the investments will move in opposite directions part of the time. In the halls of finance, that is known as how well investments correlate with one another.
- You want to combine investments to obtain the best return with the least amount of price volatility. Ideally, you will lower your margin of error every month and still receive the kind of return you need to build your wealth. If you could choose between an investment offering an annual return of 16 percent with a price fluctuation, or margin of error, of

181

24 percent, or an investment mix providing a 12 percent return with a 12 percent margin of error, which would you choose? The answer depends on how much you want to risk. Hint: Before choosing the former offering, think honestly about how you would feel if you lost nearly $2,500 on each $10,000 you invested in a single year.

Constructing an investment mix to obtain the best return with the lowest margin of error—taking into account an individual's risk parameters—is known in finance as optimizing your portfolio. (I wonder what academic coined a word as forbidding as optimization to explain a concept as simple as finding the best investment mix with the least amount of risk?)

When you mix your portfolio properly, you can boost your return and lower the monthly price hit, or risk of losses in the event you have to sell (see Table 9.2). If you

---

Table 9.2   Rebalancing Cuts Risk, Increases Return
(for ten years ending in March 1993)

Category	Annual Rate %	Annual Margin of Error %	$4,000 Grows to Over 10 Years
Group I: Buy and Hold Four Funds	10.5	± 12.7	$10,832
Group II: Rebalance 25% a year	7%	± 12.7	7,869
Group III: Rebalance for Higher Risk Adjusted Return	13.2	± 13.0	13,821
50/50 S&P 500 and Bond Index	12.9	± 11.5	13,459
S&P 500	14.4	± 17.1	15,357

were a low-risk investor who wanted some growth from stocks, but also safety, you simply could adopt one of our model portfolios. Using that, you would put 40 percent in Vanguard Index 500, 43 percent in the Scudder International Fund, 5 percent in U.S. Gold Fund, and 12 percent in a money fund. (We have eliminated the bond fund because this existing mix would have a better margin of error than a portfolio that included bonds.)

Rebalancing based on these percentages over the ten years ending in March 1993 would have given you an annual rate of return of 13.3 percent. During that same period the S&P 500 gained 14.40 percent a year. You earned 92 percent of the return on the market, but with about one third less risk.

This mix of funds give you the best return with just a tab more risk based on the annual margin of error, which is also known as the standard deviation. You earned over 13 percent a year with a margin of error of about 13. That's a lot more return than portfolios which are divided in quarters. Group I and Group II underperformed Group III or the higher risk mix and their margins of error were 12.7 percent.

Take Group III anytime. You could have bought and held the four funds for ten years. If you did, you earned 10.5 percent a year. You were diversified, but failed to maximize your return. Twenty-five percent of your money was invested in precious metals which is a highly volatile investment. This portfolio is less risky than a 100 percent stake in stocks, but the performance gets dragged down by large positions in gold and cash.

If you want to keep it simple, the 50/50 mix works well. You earn 89 percent of the return on the market with less risk. You earned 98 percent of the return on the higher risk mix of Group III, but the portfolio was 12 percent less risky.

CHAPTER 10

Market Timing Versus Buy-and-Hold Strategies

Have you ever received junk mail from stock-market timers—investment advisors who have developed computer programs that tell them when to switch between stocks and cash based on trend analysis?

If so, you may remember the pitch: usually a letter or brochure with a large photo of an extremely serious-looking financial advisor who bears a faint resemblance to Obi-wan Kenobi. In a box next to the picture, Obi-wan assures you that his investment system has returned 20 percent a year since 1982. In case you think that this is just the luck of the bull market, he has backtested his system over the past ten years and received similar results— just last week. Wow! When you're hot, you're hot.

These advisors are good salesmen. They are convincing, especially if they have amassed a good record over the past few years. It is natural to be impressed by someone who has made a few good market calls. If you are going to diversify based on your risk tolerance, however, you should ignore these stock-market mavens. Sad to say, financial research has demonstrated that stock-market timing does not work. Timers can make big profits over short periods of time—such as a few years—but the law of averages works against these systems. Using the concepts of diversification and portfolio rebalancing is a better way to invest. You manage your risks wisely and you peg your investments to meet your financial goals.

Truckloads of material offering hot investment advice is sent to investors every day. Advisory services buy mailing lists and bombard people with advice on how to earn riches in investments ranging from pork bellies to switching rapidly between stocks and money funds. Every one of these brochures shows you how much money the system has yielded in the past. You do not receive reports acknowledging how many times the system has lost money. This leads one to ask, "There must be a lot of wealthy people on the face of this earth. But if they have found the secret of stock-market success, why are they sharing it with anyone else?"

We hate to draw hasty conclusions, but it looks like it is more profitable to sell market-timing services than it is to time the market. Look at what happened when the market crashed—plenty of leading gurus lost their shirts. The "Hulbert Financial Digest," a Washington, D.C.–based newsletter that tracks the performance of market-timing investment advisors, is littered with advisory services that lost reams of money in October of 1987.

AVOID MARKET TIMING

Such debacles are the reason why we advise you to avoid market timing when you allocate assets. You want to buy for the long term, hedge your investments and set up a procedure for buying more shares when prices decline.

Mutual-funds portfolio managers hate market timers. The T. Rowe Price investment company has asked a dozen timers to leave their fund group over the past year. So has the Vanguard group. Fidelity Investments is considering charging an extra tenth of a percent redemption fee on million-dollar exchanges caused by market timers.

Timing pros give portfolio managers major headaches. When large sums of money flow into a fund as the market is rising, a manager has two choices: He or she can place the influx into cash and wait for buying opportunities—thus lowering the return—or he or she can invest at a time when stock prices are probably too high. When the market falls, money redeemed by market timers prevents portfolio managers from buying stocks at low prices. They also may be forced to sell shares, generating capital gains that are taxed. All that trading increases the transaction costs of the fund and further hurts performance.

For all that heartache, the timers' gyrations often do not seem to pay off. Constellation Growth Fund's portfolio manager Harry Hutzler, who controls assets of $140 million, reports that most timers who were in his fund were way off base during the bull market. By mid-1987, his fund was up 28 percent, but one timer took his clients' money out five times during the first seven months of the year.

SUCCESSFUL COIN FLIPPERS

Always remember that when the stock market is going up, everyone looks like a winner. Almost anyone's barber or brother-in-law can flash an impressive earnings record for the period stretching between 1982 and 1987. Market timing has come under intense criticism from both theoreticians and those who manage mutual-funds portfolios. According to research, a timing record established over a four- or five-year period is insufficient to judge whether switching between cash and equities can outperform the market averages. Over the course of decades, winning periods in the market are so far and few between that it is practically impossible to be even 75 percent correct in timing the markets successfully. Those who make the right calls over the short term generally are nothing more than successful coin flippers.

HOT OVER THE SHORT RUN

Current data reveals that over the short term, a money manager can give a boffo performance, but, over the long term—and we are talking about more than 20 years—the risk catches up with the returns and portfolios tend to fall back toward the market averages. One statistician calculated that a money manager would have to outperform the market average by two percent annually over 70 years to be considered a superstar. Is that going to happen? Probably not.

Market timers argue that their systems function as asset protection. If they pull you out of the market in time to avoid large losses, your investments will profit accordingly. Even if they are only 50 percent right in any given year, the argument goes, if those 50-percent calls save you from a severe bear market, the service is worth it.

YOU CANNOT BEAT THE AVERAGE OVER THE LONG HAUL

Suppose you have 32 money managers who time the market. Recently, they have been accurate in calling market turns about half of the time. Let's consider flipping a coin and either investing in the S&P 500 or T-bills from 1980 through 1984. If you get tails, you put money in T-bills at the beginning of the year; with heads you buy stocks. Over five years, the odds of making the correct decision every year are 32 to 1—a real long shot. The odds that one of the 32 advisors will be correct every year is about 5 to 2—that is a better bet, as long as you know in advance who that prescient individual is going to be.

Figure 10.1 **Distribution of Five-year Coin-Flip Returns***

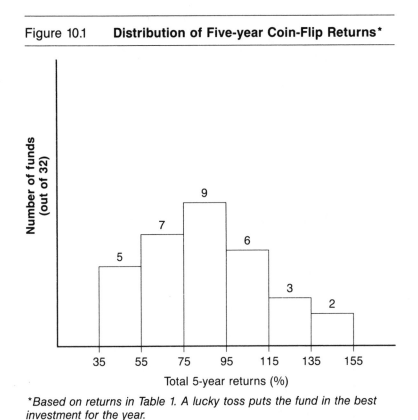

Based on returns in Table 1. A lucky toss puts the fund in the best investment for the year.

Source: *The Mutual Fund Letter,* Investment Information Services, Chicago, IL

If a timing pro were right every time (see Table 10.1), he or she would have invested in stocks in 1980, T-bills in 1981, stocks in 1982 and 1983 and T-bills in 1984. This gifted market timer would have profited at an annual rate of 20 percent, compared to a buy-and-hold gain of 15 percent. A poor timer who was wrong every year would have averaged only 6 percent. Meanwhile, a safety-conscious investor who bought T-bills would have gained a worry-free 10.93 percent annually.

Figure 10.2   **Distribution of Five-year Mutual-Funds Returns (1980 through 1984)**

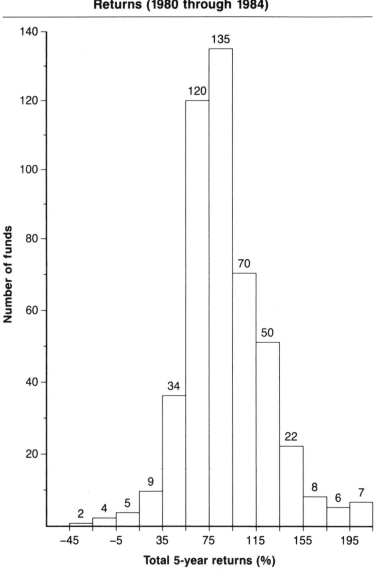

Source: *The Mutual Fund Letter,* Investment Information Services, Chicago, IL

Table 10.1   S&P 500 Versus T-bills

Year	S&P 500	T-bills
1980	32.4%	11.2
1981	−4.2	14.7
1982	21.4	10.5
1983	22.5	8.8
1984	6.3	9.8

If you plotted out the returns of our 32 coin-flipping market timers, you would see that half of them would have beaten the market average and half would have underperformed it. The average for the group was a cumulative growth of 85.2 percent, about the same return as a mutual fund with a 50-50 stock and T-bill split over the five years.

Let's look at a real-world return earned by 472 common stock funds during the five-year period in question. The distribution of the returns is similar to that of our hypothetical coin flippers. The average return for all stock funds was a cumulative 88.6 percent. Big winners such as Fidelity Magellan gained 314 percent and big losers such as 44 Wall Street Fund lost 51 percent. Only 146 funds, or 31 percent, beat the market averages. Almost as many—128 funds, or 27 percent—earned less than the return on a buy-and-hold position in T-bills. Another 250 funds, or 53 percent, performed worse than the coin flipper investing only in stocks and T-bills.

AND WHEN YOU'RE NOT YOU'RE NOT

Over short periods of time, whether you hire a coin flipper or buy and hold a stock fund, you suddenly can log impressive gains. The distribution of both sets of returns reflects that trend, for you see a large number of returns in both groups hovering around the averages. A certain percentage of investors in the market will do better than

191

the average and another percentage will do worse (this is what makes averages averages). If a manager or fund outperforms the market average over the short term, it usually is because of plain old luck. Over the long term, the performance of a managed portfolio will tend to track the averages. In other words, the longer someone assumes risk, the greater the chance that at some point it will pay off—but the greater the chance, too, that a mistake will catch up with the risk taker. Once he or she starts losing, his or her performance will be reduced and will move back to the averages.

Let's look at it this way: The market gained 99 percent over five years and a successful timing pro logged a 110-percent gain during that time. The following year, the manager's calls were less accurate; the fund made only 8 percent while the market gained 19 percent. Now our successful timer's return for the entire six years has drifted back toward the median, with a record for the period of 118 percent, the same as the market average.

CATCH THE TURNS BY STAYING FULLY INVESTED

When you buy and hold, allocate assets and rebalance your portfolio every year, you ensure that you always are fully invested to catch the turns in the market. When you combine that tactic with dollar cost averaging, you keep the cost per share below the market value, as we have shown in the previous chapters.

Buy-and-hold, low-risk investment tactics registered surprisingly good returns over the past decade. Over the ten years ending in June of 1988, a dollar-cost-averaging program in which you placed $20,000 into both the S&P 500 and the Salomon Brothers Corporate Bond Index would have grown to $61,000—representing a $41,000 profit on one of the least risky ways to invest.

Do not be misled by tales of two or three years of 20 percent profits in one fund or system. You cannot predict the future. You do not know when a booming manager's returns will start moving back to the market averages. What you do know is that the returns always do move back. The greater the long-term record of a manager, the greater the chance that if you invest now, you will start losing money because the manager's performance will regress toward the averages.

EASY WAY TO INVEST AND PROFIT

Even simple asset allocation reaps great rewards. If you maintained a 50-percent stock and bond split or 60-40 split every year over the past ten years, your investments would have grown at annual compound rates of 12.48 percent and 13.27 percent, respectively. And your portfolio would have been less volatile than the overall stock market.

GET AMNESIA

You are not going to get rich overnight, so forget about market timing and divide your portfolio to receive the maximum return you can with the least amount of risk. Remember that you might like the idea of those 25-percent gains on sizzling growth stocks, but you could lose just as much.

Here is what the late Benjamin Graham, father of modern security analysis and author of *The Intelligent Investor* and *Security Analysis,* said about market timing: "The investor can scarcely take seriously the innumerable predictions which appear almost daily and are his for the asking," Graham wrote. "Yet in many cases he pays attention to them and even acts on them. Why? Because he has been persuaded that it is important for him to form some opinion of the future course of the stock market and because he feels that the brokerage firm or service forecast is at least more dependable than his own.

"A great deal of brain power goes into this field (market forecasting) and undoubtedly some people can make money by being good stock market analysts," Graham added. "But it is absurd to think that the general public can ever make money out of market forecasts. For who will buy when the general public, at a given signal, rushes to sell out at a profit? If you expect to get rich over the years by following some system or leadership in market forecasting, you must be expecting to do what countless others are aiming at, and to be able to do it better than your numerous competitors in the market. There is no basis either in logic or in experience for assuming that any average investor can anticipate market movements more successfully than the general public of which he is himself a part."

IF YOU CAN'T BEAT 'EM, JOIN 'EM

Certain financial studies show that over the long term it is almost impossible to beat the market by constantly shifting assets between money funds or T-bills and stocks. Robert H. Jeffrey, president of The Jeffrey Company, an investment firm in Columbus, Ohio, believes that the risks of making poor timing decisions outweigh the rewards.

"Over a short period of time, like five years, a market timer may show good performance," says Jeffrey. "But I don't think timing works because the rewarding periods in the market are far and few between. If you could find a timer who was correct 75 percent of the time, it would be a good deal."

Jeffrey's position is based on his 1984 study, "The Folly of Stock Market Timing," published in the *Harvard Business Review.* By looking at the best and worst possible returns that could have been made on the

S&P 500 compared to investing in 90-day T-bills, he found that market timing stood a greater chance of losing money than making profits. To be 100 percent correct about the outlook for the market meant to be out of T-bills and in stocks every time the market moved up—to be 100 percent wrong meant always to be fully invested in the S&P 500 when it was declining.

BEING RIGHT PART OF THE TIME DOES NOT BEAT THE MARKET

The results of Jeffrey's study showed that the best anyone could have done being 100 percent correct was a 15.9 percent annual return from 1975 through 1982. The worst would have been an annual loss of 11 percent. A simple buy-and-hold strategy in stocks gained 5.7 percent a year. The spread between the worst possible outcome and the buy and hold was 16.7 percent. A timer who was 50 percent correct would have made about 1.5 percent during that period—one who was 75 percent correct would have made 7.5 percent. As a result, Jeffrey concludes that there is a greater chance of losing money using market timing than of making superior returns.

From 1926 through 1982, Jeffrey found that market-timing performance fell between the worst possible outcome and the best. Because there were only ten quarters (three-month time periods) over the past 56 years responsible for boosting the returns on stocks, the chances of picking upturns in the market were slim. In statistical terms, he found that the probabilities of catching 100 percent of the upturns in the market are only 4 in 1,000. A timer who is only right about half the time has a great chance of losing money.

Other research supports Jeffrey's position. One study found that after paying taxes on trades, investors earned $1,000 less by trading on a moving average than they would have earned if they had bought and held an investment for ten years. Mark Hulbert found that over a 2.5 year period ending in mid 1988, timing pros under-performed the market because after they switched out of stocks to avoid losses, they returned at higher prices. In another study, he concluded that timers who made the fewest switches over the past five years beat the market averages. They were fully invested and caught 100 per-cent of the rising market.

In a study similar to Jeffrey's, Professors Jess Chua and Richard Woodward of the University of Calgary also found that the odds of timing the market correctly over the long term were slim. If a timer was right 70 percent of the time—which would be a prodigious feat—he or she still would barely outperform the market averages. From 1926 through 1983, investors would have earned an annual rate of return of 18.2 percent if they were 100 percent correct in switching between T-bills and stocks. A buy and hold on the S&P 500 during the same time period grew at an annual rate of 11.8 percent. If a timer was only 70 percent correct in switching, the annual return dropped to 12.1 percent. If a timer was right half the time, the annual gain would be only 8.1 percent.

The lesson to be learned from this chapter is that there is no get-rich-quick way to make money in the stock market. Over ten years, you might be invested in a fund such as Fidelity Magellan that is up 1,000 percent. But when you invest, you really never know when the law of averages will catch up with you.

BEAR SCARES

Over the long run, investment fundamentals determine the value of a share of common stock. However, in the short run, fear and greed can drive stock prices well above or below their fair values. Fear and greed can also result in financial disaster to the investors who give in to these emotions. Fear can cause investors to park their money in "safe" money market funds, bank accounts, or certificates of deposit. As the old adage goes: "It's better to be safe than sorry." However, after the payment of taxes, money parked in these vehicles for long periods of time turns out not to be safe at all. That's because inflation eats into capital to such an extent that investment wealth actually shrinks over time. And the longer money stays parked in these vehicles, the greater the losses become. On the other hand, greed can cause individuals to adopt investment postures that are so risky that setbacks can widen out their entire nest egg.

DIVERSIFY

So what's an investor to do? The answer is simple: Don't give in to either emotion. Build a well-diversified portfolio that contains no more risk than you can tolerate and vow to be a long-term investor. Resolve to maintain that portfolio and gradually make changes as economic conditions warrant. This advice, or course, is easy to dispense but hard to swallow. However, a look at some numbers should increase your resolve.

Take the stock market during the last 50 years for example. During this period, common stocks as represented by Standard & Poor's 500 Index returned 12.9 percent compounded annually. One thousand dollars invested in this hypothetical portfolio at the beginning of 1942 would have grown to $464,540 by the end of 1992. Of course, the value of that portfolio would have suffered some bumps and bruises along the way. During the 1973–74 bear market, for example, the value of the portfolio would have tumbled slightly more than 46 percent. During the three months September through November 1987, the value of the portfolio would have sunk by nearly 30 percent.

However, if you invest in the stock market, you are going to spend a considerable amount of time watching the value of your portfolio decline. Here's a bit of what equity investors have suffered during the last 50 years. Since 1942, there have been 22 declines in stock prices of 8 percent or more, 18 declines of 10 percent or more, 11 setbacks of 15 percent or more, 6 plunges of 20 percent or more, and 3 in excess of 30 percent. During these 22 declining periods, the stock market spent 171 months going down. In other words, during the last 50 years, the stock market has spent 30 percent of the time in retreat. These sharp market reversals have occurred, on average, every two and one-half years. And these periods of decline have lasted from one to 21 months with the average being 7.8 months.

5 BEST AND 5 WORST PERIODS IN THE MARKET

Market timers are quick to point out that they *can* help investors maneuver the market's obstacle course and improve their investment returns. The inference is that by dodging bear markets portfolio volatility is reduced and profits are enhanced. This is a very powerful statement. It implies that market timers can both reduce risk and increase investment return. That, of course, is subject to considerable debate. In fact, market timers expose investors to more risk than exists in a buy-and-hold strategy. The following example illustrates why.

We identified the market's five best and five worst performing years since 1942. We then computed the value of $1 assuming that investors were able to dodge the worst performing years. Of course, investment performance was enhanced. By dodging the market's worst performing years, the value of $1 invested in 1942 would have grown to $998.20 by the end of 1992. That's a $533.60 improvement over a buy-and-hold strategy, or slightly more than twice that of the passive strategy. On the other hand, a completely inept market timer who managed to stay *in* the market during its *worst* five years but stayed out of the market during its five *best* years would have seen the value of $1 invested in 1942 increase to only $85.60. That's less than one-fiftieth the value of a buy-and-hold strategy. In other words, there's more to be lost by being absolutely wrong than there is to gain by being absolutely correct about the stock market's future direction.

Here are a few more examples. A market timer who happened to dodge the market's five worst years but also stayed out the market during its single best year would have attained a portfolio valued at $654.06, or about a 50 percent improvement over a buy-and-hold strategy. However, the timer who was out of the market during its worst five years but missed two of its best years would have failed to keep pace with a buy-and-hold strategy. In other words, make only a few timing errors and your long-run return will suffer.

If you were lucky enough to be out of the stock market during its five worst years during the last 50 years, you would have increased your annual return from 12.9 percent (for a buy-and-hold strategy) to 14.6 percent. On the other hand, if you were unlucky and managed to be out of the market during its five best performing years during this period, your annual return would have been trimmed to 9.7 percent. In other words, you have much more to lose by being out of the stock market than being in it.

Market timing *can* increase investment returns. However, even a few timing errors can cause investment returns to fall below those obtained by a passive buy-and-hold strategy. And the odds favor a reduction rather than an enhancement of portfolio value. In other words, attempting to time the market increases rather than decreases investment risk.

While it's painful to watch the value of your portfolio shrink during a bear market, it's better to stay the course than cut and run. As seen in the accompanying examples, there is more to lose by missing a bull market than there is to gain by dodging a bear market. Bear markets are a fact of investment life and you must learn to live with them. If you can't tolerate a severe market plunge, then spread your capital around. For example, a portfolio containing one-third common stocks, one-third bonds and one-third money market mutual funds would have declined by less than 12 percent during 1973–74, the worst bear market in the last half century.

CHAPTER 11

Retirement Savings Plans

POT OF GOLD AT THE END OF THE RAINBOW

By the time most of us retire, if we have been faithful savers, our retirement kitty may hold $350,000 or more. This would provide a retiree with about $40,000 a year in income, including Social Security payments. This sounds like a lot of money, but, on second thought, it could cost $50 just to make a cross-country telephone call to an old retired pal.

We cannot short-circuit inflation. In 20 years, at the moderate inflation rate of five percent, a dollar will be worth half of what it is today. Everything will cost twice as much—a couple's weekly $60 worth of groceries will cost $120 and so on.

Placing money in an IRA or another type of retirement savings account can provide you with an edge over inflation in several ways. Retirement contributions are tax-deductible, so you save money now by paying less income tax.

TAX-DEFERRED GROWTH

Retirement savings also grow tax-deferred until you take distributions when you retire. This deferment makes your retirement account your very own tax shelter and the savings can be staggering. If you place $2,000 a year in an IRA that earned eight percent annually, you would have a retirement kitty of $90,853 at the end of 20 years. (Assuming you are in the 28 percent tax bracket, though, and the investment was taxable, your money would be pruned to only $75,817 by the Internal Revenue Service [IRS]).

One rule of thumb is that you should plan to draw about 70 to 80 percent of your current income from your retirement savings, in addition to Social Security. If you currently make $30,000 a year, you will need to accumulate $224,164 in a retirement kitty that earns eight percent a year by the time you reach age 65. This sum will provide you with an annual income of $22,500. If you make $50,000 a year, you will need to amass $373,607 to provide you with an annual income of $37,500. If you currently make $70,000 a year, it will take $523,050 to provide you with your target annual income of $52,500.

HOW LONG YOUR MONEY WILL LAST

You should be in a lower tax bracket when you draw your pension, so you will pay lower taxes on distributions than you did on your income. Because only a small percentage of your investment is received every year in the form of income, the remaining money still grows tax-deferred. You must determine how long your money will last even while you are withdrawing income from the investment pool. Too many people think they must live off only their investment income. You can, however, withdraw some of your principal every year and your money still will go a long way.

- If you took six percent out of your retirement fund every year and the investment earned just four percent, your money still would last 27 years.
- If you took an annual payout of seven percent and the investment earned six percent, your money would last 33 years.
- If you took eight percent out a year and the investment earned six percent, your money would last 23 years. If you earned seven percent, your money would last 29 years.
- At a nine percent payout rate, your money would last 17 years, if you earned a five percent return. Assuming the same payout rate, your money would last 19 years, 22 years, and 28 years, if the account earned six, seven and eight percent, respectively.
- Assuming you took a ten percent annual payout, your money would last 16, 18, and 21 years, if you earned six, seven, and eight percent on the account, respectively.

For example, you, aged 70, and your spouse, aged 67, have a life expectancy of 20 more years based on IRS rules. It might be comforting to know how much your retirement fund will pay you over your remaining years.

INCOME BASED ON LIFE EXPECTANCY

Tax law requires that your retirement money be drawn down to zero based on estimated life expectancies. While you can recalculate your life expectancy every year once you retire, the rules essentially mean that you must withdraw one-twentieth or five percent of the total in your retirement pool in the first year, one-tenth or 10 percent by the 10th year and 100 percent by the 20th.

If you have a healthy sum in your account—$250,000, for example—you can rest assured you always will have a base of retirement funds. If the retirement account earns eight percent a year, even with the required amount of withdrawals, the fund will pay out $638,115 in income over 20 years. If the earnings rate was ten percent, the payout would be $827,540. At 12 percent, the fund would pay out $1,081,475 in income over 20 years.

RETIREMENT PLANS: TAX-FREE SAVINGS

Several types of retirement plans let you save money tax-deferred until you retire. Individual Retirement Accounts (IRAs) and 401(k) salary-reduction pension plans are two of the most popular. We will discuss the specifics of these accounts later in this chapter.

IRAs are self-directed plans. With an IRA, you can choose to invest in individual stocks and bonds, mutual funds and bank Certificates of Deposit (CDs). Company 401(k) pension plans let employees invest in a choice of stock and bond mutual funds. The amount contributed reduces taxable wages reported to the IRS.

More complicated company pension plans do exist. Defined-benefit and defined-contribution plans also may invest in a stable of mutual funds or fixed-income products. The amounts contributed or paid out at retirement, however, are predetermined.

IRA RULES

Any person who earned income and does not deduct money from his or her pay and place it in a company pension plan can make tax-deductible contributions to an IRA. Single people can place $2,000 into an IRA and receive a dollar-for-dollar deduction on their income tax. Married couples who file joint returns can salt away $4,000, or $2,250 if one spouse does not work.

If you already are a participant in a pension plan, then you are limited on your tax-deductible IRA contributions. If you are single and make less than $25,000 a year, your

$2,000 annual contributions are deductible. Singles and heads of households who make between $25,000 and $35,000 receive partial deductions. You lose about $1 in deductions for every $5 of income, and no deductions are permitted on incomes of more than $35,000.

Married couples who file joint returns, with incomes of $40,000 or less, can deduct all of their $4,000 in IRA contributions. For couples who make between $40,001 and $50,000, $1 of deduction is phased out for every $5 of income. If the couple makes more than $50,000, their IRA contributions are nondeductible.

To keep your tax deductions, you must follow some pretty stiff rules. If you withdraw money from your IRA before you reach the age of $59\frac{1}{2}$, you must pay a ten-percent penalty and the withdrawal is considered taxable income. You must begin receiving distributions by April 1 after the year you reach the age of $70\frac{1}{2}$. You can withdraw money from your IRA before $59\frac{1}{2}$, but you must roll the money back into the same or another IRA account within 60 days or face the early withdrawal fine and income tax on the distribution.

SALARY-REDUCTION PLANS

401(k) pension plans are fast becoming the most popular company pension plan in use today. Industry statistics reveal that more than 31 percent of all American workers were enrolled in 401(k) plans the past year. By the end of the decade, analysts predict that almost 90 percent of all workers will be enrolled in these plans.

Known as "salary-reduction" plans, 401(k) plans are tax-qualified profit-sharing plans that include a cash or deferred arrangement. Employees can elect to have part of their wages contributed to the plan—usually six to ten percent of their gross income. Their taxable income is reduced by the amount of their contributions. Employers may make tax deductible matching contributions to the retirement plan. In tax years 1987 and beyond, pretax employee contributions are limited to $7,000 a year plus an inflation adjustment. Today, you can put $8,994 into your 401(k) plan. And don't forget your employer's contributions. Some companies match 50 cents on the dollar or more. So if you invested the maximum and your boss kicked in money, you would have almost $18,000 invested for retirement.

Employees also can make after-tax contributions to the plans. They should have a wide choice of investment options to choose from, depending on the company. Most mutual funds offer investors a choice of a money fund, government and corporate bond funds and stock funds ranging from growth to income. The employer's contributions generally are vested after ten years. In plan years beginning after December 31, 1988, employer contributions are vested after five years, according to the Tax Reform Act of 1986. In addition, employees can begin to withdraw funds without penalty from the 401(k) plan when they reach the age of $59\frac{1}{2}$.

FLEXIBLE PLANS

These 401(k) plans are flexible pension plans that can be tailor-made to meet a particular company's needs. For example:

- Thrift plans enable the employees to contribute a portion of their pay; the employer may match contributions. The funds are held in trust. On retirement, the employee has a pension fund that represents the accumulated earnings from both his or her and the employer's contributions.
- Profit-Sharing Plans. The employee makes tax-deferred contributions and the employer makes contributions based on a portion of the firm's year-end profits. The employee has the option of taking the

employers' contributions in cash but must pay ordinary income tax on the money if he or she does so.

- Stand-Alone Plans. These are 401(k) plans where the employer makes no contributions.
- Cafeteria Plans. These 401(k) plans also may include life insurance, medical and dental insurance, disability insurance, legal services and child care.

TRADITIONAL PENSION PLANS AND RETIREMENT SAVINGS

In addition to the popular 401(k) plan, corporations still can set up traditional pension plans with mutual-funds investment options. Pension plans come in two basic forms: defined-benefit and defined-contribution plans. Typically, larger corporations with more than $10 million in retirement funds will have the pension funds managed by a mutual-funds company's investment division. This division will not invest the funds in the firm's stable of retail mutual-funds products: they will create a separate fund exclusively for the firm based on its specific investment objectives.

DEFINED BENEFITS WHEN YOU RETIRE

Defined-benefit plans are used by large corporations, unions, and government agencies. With a defined-benefit plan, the retirement provision is decided on in advance, using a flat benefit or career income–average formula. As a result, these plans reduce the uncertainty about how much a retirement account will grow to; they guarantee employees a specific income when they retire. The annual benefit from this type of plan, according to the Tax Reform Act of 1986, should be the lesser of $90,000 or 100 percent of an employee's average compensation for his or her three highest earnings years, indexed to the inflation rate.

OR YOU CAN MAKE PREDETERMINED CONTRIBUTIONS

Defined-contribution plans are the reverse of defined-benefit plans. A 401(k) plan is a type of defined-contribution plan. With this system, an employer and/or an employee make monthly contributions into a fund and the earnings accumulate. The maximum amount that an employer can contribute is the lesser of 25 percent of an employee's compensation or $30,000 per year, indexed to inflation. A thrift plan, which is a type of contribution plan, enables employees to contribute annually six percent of earned income into the plan. On retirement, the employee will receive monthly income based on the accumulated principal and the interest in the account.

Simplified Employee Pension (SEP). SEPs are employee-sponsored plans that are considered a special type of IRA. Employer's contributions are limited to the lesser of $30,000 or 15 percent of compensation, indexed to inflation.

Self-Employed Keogh Plans. Self-employed individuals, sole proprietors, and partners can set up a retirement plan for themselves and their employees. (By law, the employer who sets up a Keogh must make the retirement plan available to employees.) Keoghs either can take the form of defined-benefit or defined-contribution plans.

LIFE-INSURANCE PRODUCTS COST TOO MUCH

Everyone needs five times their current annual income to cushion the family in the event of an unforeseen death. You must have life insurance. As an investment vehicle, unfortunately, insurance falls far short. You pay too much in commissions and other fees to make life insurance a worthwhile investment.

Life insurance formerly was one of those ho-hum things that you had to have to protect the family in the event of a breadwinner's death. Insurance benefits substituted for the lost income of the wage earner. Now that has all changed. Insurance companies now are offering enticing products and the new tax laws make cash buildup on policies one of the few tax shelters around. When you buy a life-insurance policy, part of the premium pays for death benefits and part goes into a savings or investment account which is designated as the cash value of the policy. When you buy term insurance, there is no cash value. You buy just the death benefits.

In the old days, the only kinds of insurance available were term and whole life. When inflation soared, interest rates rose and then the stock market took off, consumers demanded better returns from their life-insurance policies.

TERM INSURANCE COVERS BASIC NEEDS

Term insurance was purchased to provide limited protection for a specified period of time. Nothing was paid to beneficiaries of term insurance if the breadwinner outlived the policy—unless it was rolled over into a new permanent life policy. If death occurred during the time the policy was in force, the beneficiaries collected the policy's face amount or death benefit. For a few hundred dollars a year, a breadwinner could insure his or her family for a hefty sum. Unlike other types of life insurance, however, term insurance does not generate investment income or cash value.

Some term insurance policies are renewable if your health changes. Each time you renew the policy for a new period, however, your cost increases. Some term policies are convertible. You can switch to a permanent life insurance policy that has cash-value buildup.

WHOLE LIFE

Whole life was bought by those who wanted permanent life insurance plus savings. Monthly payments or premiums fund a specific death benefit, and the payments also earn interest or cash value over the years. The most common type of whole life is called straight life. You pay the same premium every year for as long as you live. The premiums can be higher than those of term insurance, but smaller than a renewable term policy. Also, with some policies you can pay premiums for a 20-year period. When you reach 65, for example, the death benefits would equal the face amount of the insurance plus the cash value. In addition, the interest buildup or cash value of the policy often is used as the source of a low-cost loan. Policy borrowing has become more expensive over the years; today, it could cost you ten percent or more to borrow from your policy.

UNIVERSAL LIFE

Universal life was created a few years ago when interest rates skyrocketed. It is essentially a whole-life or permanent policy that lets you make flexible premium payments. Policyholders who have pressing financial needs or limited income can vary the amount and timing of their premium payments. Payments are invested by the insurance company in the short-term money and bond markets. As a result, the amount of death benefits above the amount guaranteed by the insurance company varies with the amount of the premium payments and the interest earned on the account.

VARIABLE LIFE

Variable-life insurance offers consumers a different twist. As with whole life, you receive permanent insurance coverage. With variable life, however, the policy-holder assumes the investment risk instead of having the insurance company assume it. You have a choice of investing in a money-market account, a bond fund, and various types of stock mutual funds. Because the amount of the cash buildup changes with the performance of the stocks or bonds, the earnings and death benefits of the policy above a floor amount guaranteed by the insurance company will vary.

SINGLE-PREMIUM LIFE

With single-premium life insurance, you make one premium payment, which could be as little as $5,000. You receive about five times that amount in death benefits and your money earns a fixed rate based on the prevailing market. Or you can invest in a stable of mutual funds with the hope of zipping up the cash value of your policy.

Today, insurance companies are heavily promoting variable-life insurance as a tax-free way to invest. The buildup on the cash value is not taxable, even when you borrow from your policy. The sales pitch is that you receive life insurance protection for the family and you can allocate assets across a wide range of investments to earn higher returns than fixed-rate whole-life policies earn. Some of the larger insurance companies even employ money managers who will decide where your cash values are invested based on current economic conditions.

TOO MANY FEES

Life-insurance salespeople stress that you receive tax-free accumulation on the cash value or investment portion of your policy. What insurance people will show you is a chart demonstrating the after-tax return on stocks, bonds, and T-bills compared to the cash-value buildup on your insurance policy. And voila! What do you think

211

happens? You receive a better after-tax return on insurance than you do in the stock market. Sound familiar? These sales people are just as bad as the market timers we mentioned earlier in the book.

What the insurance salesperson did not tell you was that you must pay more than 20 percent in commissions over the first few years of the policy, 6 percent in fees for administrative costs and mortality fees, a 2 percent state excise tax on premium payments, back-end surrender charges for the first ten years of the policy's life and $1/2$ percent management fees on all of your mutual-funds investments.

RAW DEAL WHEN YOU BORROW

You also get a raw deal when you borrow from one of these variable-life policies. The reason you put your insurance money in this type of policy was so that your investments would earn more money than you would earn with a policy that pays a fixed rate. If you borrow from a variable-life policy, though, the insurance company will take your cash value and transfer the money to an account that pays a fixed rate of interest—about two percent below your loan rate. Your cash value now is collateral for the loan. The insurance company does not want to see their collateral decline in value if the stock market takes a dive. If the stock market is on the rise, you lose out on the growth because your money now is in a fixed-rate account paying about eight percent interest.

Enough said about life-insurance products as investments. You must protect your family and the cash-value investments enable you to borrow money at a below-market rate without ever paying back the loan. Shop around and find a policy that provides you with the best returns at the lowest rates.

A QUESTION TO ASK BEFORE YOU BUY

Before you buy life insurance, you should ask yourself the following question:

Why you are buying insurance rather than salting away money in municipal bonds or IRAs? Experts say that you should buy only as much insurance as you need to protect your family. A rough estimate is that you should have at least five times your annual income in life insurance.

Compare variable-life policies. Ask for written material on the policies, not just a brochure. Compare a number of policies using this checklist:

- What are the sales loads? Front-end insurance commissions can range from as little as 3 percent to as much as 50 percent. Financial planners may charge $500 for a no-load policy. You should compare the investment returns net, after fees. Ask your agent, financial planner, or accountant to calculate the Internal Rate of Return (IRR) on your life insurance policy illustration's cash surrender value. The IRR will tell you what you really earn net of commissions, the cost of insurance, and fees. If the IRR on your policy's cash surrender value is more than 2.5 percent, its a bum deal. Look for a lower cost policy.
- Compare the cost of term insurance, underwriting a medical examination, and annual administrative fees. These fees could lop six percent off the top of your investment's return.
- Compare surrender charges. If you cash in your policy early, you will have to pay a surrender fee in addition to paying income tax on the earnings on the policy's cash value. When you withdraw money from an insurance policy, the amount in excess of

the sum of the premiums paid is considered taxable income.

- Compare similar policies' interest adjusted cost indexes. This index shows you the cost per $1,000 of insurance. The lower the index number the lower the cost.

CHAPTER 12

The Changing World
of Mutual Funds

Everyone is getting into the mutual fund business these days. Over the past three years the industry changed dramatically. Now we can invest in no-load funds without paying transaction fees at discount brokerage firms. Banks sell funds. Insurance companies have teamed up with fund groups and offer variable annuities to people who want a tax-deferred investment until they retire.

ANOTHER BROKERAGE FIRM RIP-OFF

Not to be left out, many brokerage firms have reduced their front-end mutual fund loads. But don't worry. Brokerage firms have come up with a new way to fleece you. Avoid their wrap accounts like the plague. The reason: With a wrap account, a stock-broker hires a professional to manage your stock, bond, or fund investments. You'll pay a whopping 2 to 3 percent annual fee. You are guaranteed to under-perform the markets. You are better off subscribing to a no-load mutual fund newsletter for $100.

SOME CALL THEMSELVES FINANCIAL PLANNERS

We also have an entirely new group of professional advisors. Over the past ten years, the financial planning profession has grown tremendously. There are now over 25,000 financial planners in this country. Some are good. Some are bad. If you find a good one, he or she will help you with insurance, investment, retirement, and estate planning.

BEST DEAL: NO TRANSACTION FEES ACCOUNTS

You can consolidate all of your no-load funds in one account these days. Charles Schwab, the San Francisco-based discount brokerage firm, pioneered the concept of No Transaction Fee (NTF) mutual fund accounts a couple of years ago. Now others have jumped on the bandwagon. Jack White & Company and Fidelity Investment's discount brokerage firm have NTF programs.

HOW IT WORKS

You open an account with the brokerage firm and fill out the paperwork to set up an NTF account. You can have existing funds transferred into your account by filling out and returning a transfer form. Normally, you pay .6 percent to .9 percent every time you buy and sell a fund in your discount brokerage account. No more. It's free. At Schwab you have a choice of investing in 180 no-load funds. You have a choice of about the same number of funds at White & Co. and Fidelity.

You can invest in brand name fund groups like Janus, Dreyfus, Founders, Stein Roe, Invesco, and Neuberger & Berman with Schwab.

At White, you can invest in fund groups such as Blanchard, Value Line, and Gateway.

Fidelity Investments is getting into the act. At the time of this writing, Fidelity Investments is planning to offer a stable of NTF funds that includes Gabelli Funds, Jones & Babson, Benham Group, Scudder Stevens & Clark, T. Rowe Price, and the Vanguard Group of Funds.

There are a number of advantages to NTF accounts. They include the following:

- You can invest in funds with a single phone call.
- You get one monthly statement.
- Liquidity. If you need cash, you can write a check off your money fund.
- Venturesome investors can buy funds on margin.
- You can have your dividends and capital gains automatically reinvested.
- Your trades are automatically swept into your money fund.
- You have access to a representative 24 hours a day.
- If you have an IRA account you also get a break. You don't pay an IRA maintenance fee and can invest in the same group of funds transaction-fee free with an account worth $10,000 or more.

VARIABLE ANNUITIES

Consumers have invested almost $60 billion in variable annuities to date. Variable annuities are mutual funds wrapped in insurance products. Variable annuity death benefit guarantees also appeal to risk-averse investors. A variable annuity is an insurance contract that lets you invest in stock and bond mutual funds. The insurance part of the annuity is the death benefit guarantee. If you die, you are guaranteed that your beneficiaries receive the money you contributed or the current value of the annuity, whichever is higher.

Variable annuities are also popular because you get a tax break. With annuities, your money grows tax-deferred until withdrawn. That makes them hot products today. Who wants to pay higher taxes? So tax-deferred investments like annuities are popular—your money can grow tax-free up until age 85, the age at which most insurance companies require withdrawals.

INVESTMENT OPTIONS

You can make lump-sum or regular payments into an annuity and the money can grow tax-deferred. After age $59^{1}/_{2}$, you can take a lump-sum distribution from the variable annuity or receive monthly payments for life by annuitizing the contract.

You have a lot of investment options when you buy a variable annuity. You can invest in money funds, U.S. and overseas stock and bond funds, precious metals funds, and real estate funds. In addition, you can switch among funds or diversify your investments without having to pay capital gains taxes on the transactions. By contrast, every time you buy or sell a fund in a taxable account and make a profit, Uncle Sam collects his due.

What makes variable annuities even more enticing lately is that a few no-load mutual fund companies are teaming up with insurance companies to offer lower-cost variable annuities.

HIGH FEES—SO SHOP AROUND

Before you rush out to stash a bundle of money in a variable annuity, you need to shop around. If you buy the wrong product, you can get stung by high annual fees and redemption charges. The average variable annuity socks you with 2 percent in annual charges.

Regardless of the annuity's fee structure, you already pay the piper to Uncle Sam if you redeem annuity proceeds early. A person under age $59^1/_2$ would pay a 10 percent fine and income taxes on the earnings portion of the annuity withdrawal.

Although your money grows tax-free until withdrawal in an annuity, there is no free lunch. Variable annuities are high-cost products. According to Morningstar's Variable Annuity/Life Performance Report, you pay substantial fees when you invest. The average variable annuity hits you with a 2.26 percent annual charge, which is broken down as follows: A 1.26 percent annual mortality and expense charge; a .75 percent mutual fund expense charge; plus a $25 annual record and maintenance fee which translates into another .25 percent charge on a $10,000 investment.

In addition to high annual fees, most annuities assess back-end surrender charges ranging from 5 to 9 percent. Each year the surrender charge drops one percent until it is diminished. Some contracts permit partial withdrawals of up to 10 percent of the value of the contract or 10 percent of the principal. However, you are typically charged the lesser of $25 or 2 percent of the amount withdrawn for that privilege.

Why the high cost? The mortality and expense charges are a source of revenue for the insurance company. The chances of the insurance company having to pay off on a death benefit are estimated to be less than one in one thousand. In addition, brokers and financial planners are paid up to 6 percent commissions out of the mortality and expense charges. Higher fund management fees are a source of revenue to the fund companies. Back-end surrender charges also are used to compensate agents and financial planners.

The impact of annuity expenses is considerable. For example, in a worst-case scenario in which an annuity is surrendered by someone under age 59½, the investor would lose substantial income. Assuming that a $10,000 variable annuity grew at an annual rate of 8 percent over eight years, the annuitant's money grows to just $13,577. That's based on 2 percent annual annuity fees, a 1 percent surrender charge, a 10 percent IRS fine, and a 28 percent income tax on the annuity's earnings. As a result, the money grew at an annual return of just 3.9 percent over the eight years.

THE BEST DEALS

Fortunately, there are a couple of low-cost variable annuity products on the market. The Vanguard Group of Investment Companies' Variable Annuity Plan and the Scudder Group of Mutual Funds' Horizon Plan are sold directly to investors. These two no-load fund groups can reduce their insurance charges and eliminate surrender fees because they don't pay sales commissions to brokers and financial planners.

Scudder's Horizon Plan/Charter National Life Insurance Co. (800-225-2470) variable annuity product, with total assets of $150 million, offers annuitants a choice of investing in five equity funds, two fixed-income funds, and a fixed-rate account. There is no surrender charge or maintenance fee. Depending on the fund, annuitants pay just 1.36 percent in total annuity charges which includes a .70 percent mortality and expense charge and an average .66 percent fund management fee. The fund management fee is .63 percent for the U.S. equity, bond, and money funds. You'll pay more, though, if you invest in the international stock fund, which has a management fee of 1.31 percent.

The Vanguard's Variable Annuity Plan/National Home Life Assurance Co. (800-622-7447), with assets of

$500 million, offers investors a money fund, balanced fund, and a bond or equity index fund. Mortality and expense charges are .55 percent and management fees range from .32 to .42 percent. Depending on the fund, the total cost of the annuity ranges from .87 percent for the equity or bond index funds to .97 percent if you invest in the balanced fund. The total cost for the money fund is .55 percent. There is also a $25 annual maintenance charge which translates into an additional .25 percent expense on a $10,000 investment.

SHOPPING FOR A FINANCIAL PLANNER

Many investors seek the help of financial planners to set up a financial game plan. Our advice: Either do it yourself or find an experienced financial advisor.

There are no state or federal laws regulating financial planners. So if you plan to use one, shop around carefully. You want someone with at least a college degree in business and finance and several years of experience as an insurance agent, broker, or certified public accountant.

What will a financial planner do for you? Planners look at your entire financial picture—your net worth, your cash flow, and your retirement, insurance, tax, and estate needs. They then develop a game plan to help you meet your goals.

What do they charge? Some planners charge commissions. Other charge a flat fee. Some charge both fees and commissions.

Commission-based planners don't charge you for a financial plan. Then you buy load funds and life insurance from them.

Fee-based planners may charge as little as $500 to over $2,000 for their services.

Of course the combo-planners charge you too. Depending on the service, you might pay commission for life insurance and mutual fund investments or flat fees for a financial plan and investment management.

HOW TO FIND A GOOD FINANCIAL PLANNER

Ask for referrals from other professionals. Once you find a planner, ask for references. Also check with the Better Business Bureau, your state's consumer affairs department, or with the Securities & Exchange Commission to see if any complaints have been filed against the financial planner.

Be sure to check a financial planner's professional designation. A Certified Financial Planner (CFP) has completed course work and passed a national examination on all areas of financial planning. The CFP is awarded to individuals by the College of Financial Planning, Denver, CO.

A Chartered Life Underwriter (CLU) and a Chartered Financial Consultant (ChFC) are awarded to individuals with training in life insurance and financial planning by the American College, Bryn Mawr, PA.

Certified Public Accountants (CPAs) also do financial planning. A CPA candidate must have a bachelor's degree and have worked for an accounting firm for at least two years. CPAs must pass a national exam, but they are licensed by the state where they practice. Some CPAs are also Accredited Personal Financial Planning Strategists (APFS). That means that the CPA passed an examination in financial planning administered by the American Institute of Certified Public Accountants.

For free information on how to find and select a financial planner, call either the Institute of Certified Financial Planning at 800-282-7526 or the International Association for Financial Planning at 800-945-IAFP.

CONCLUSION

When you invest in mutual funds, or any type of investment, you have to look at the whole picture. Investing should be one part of a financial game plan that includes retirement, insurance, and estate planning. So, before you invest, either meet with a financial advisor or do your homework and evaluate your needs and goals.

CONCLUSION

DIVERSIFY! DIVERSIFY! DIVERSIFY!

If you learn one thing from this book, it is to divide up your investments to reduce the risk of losing too much money. Even if you keep a one-third stock, bond, and money-fund split, you are taking responsibility for your investment's well being. Even with this split you could expect your money to double about every nine years. If you split up the pie more scientifically to receive the best return with the least amount of risk, quite possibly you could see your wealth double in seven years.

YOU CAN'T PLEAD INSANITY
FOR A PARKING TICKET

When things are going good, people forget about risk. All they see are dollar signs. They are like the guy who went to traffic court and pleaded insanity for a traffic ticket. He told the judge he must be crazy to park in the passing lane on West Wacker Drive in Chicago. The judge did not buy this and fined the fellow $200 for reckless driving.

ALL GREAT BULL MARKETS END

The stock market, at the time of this writing, made back three fourths of its losses since the October 1987 crash.

Now talk is of the "Bull Market of the Century," by investment purveyors. Stocks could go higher, but no one knows for sure how long the party will last. Eventually, this seven-year economic expansion will end. We could see another 25+ percent decline in stocks, and those who forget to diversify could get burned again.

GET IN A GOOD POSITION NOW

Position yourself now and split your investments among U.S. stocks and bonds, overseas securities, and precious metals as an inflation hedge. If you do not have $50,000 to $100,000 or more to buy individual securities, consider investing in mutual funds. You can invest as little as $1,000 in a mutual fund. For that you receive professional management, diversification, a stable of mutual funds to pick from, and low-cost investments. Most no-load mutual funds have no up-front sales charges, hidden 12b-1 fees and no back-end charges. You pay between one-half and one percent in management fees, but that is a lot cheaper than paying your stockbroker.

SELECT TOP NO-LOAD MUTUAL-FUND FAMILIES

Several no-load fund families are on the market with a stable of attractive mutual funds. Some of the biggest fund families with top performing funds include Benham Management, Palo Alto, Calif.; Boston Company, Boston, Mass.; Bull & Bear Group, New York, N.Y.; Calvert Asset Management, Bethesda, Md.; The Evergreen Group, Harrison, N.Y.; Fidelity Investment, Boston, Mass.; Invesco, Denver, Colo.; Jones & Babson, Kansas City, Mo.; Lexington Funds, Saddle Brook, N.J.; Neuberger & Berman, New York, N.Y.; SAFECO Funds, Seattle, Wash.; Stein Roe & Farnham, Chicago, Ill.; T. Rowe Price, Baltimore Md.; Twentieth Century Investors, Kansas City, Mo.; Janus Group of Funds, Denver, Colo.;

United Services Advisors, San Antonio, Tex.; Strong Group of Mutual Funds, Milwaukee, Wisc.; USAA Investment Management, San Antonio, Tex.; Value Line, Inc., New York, N.Y.; and the Vanguard Group, Valley Forge, Pa.

DO YOUR HOMEWORK

If you are interested in starting an asset-allocation program, go to the public library and ask for a mutual-funds directory that lists toll free telephone numbers and addresses. Write or call the funds and ask for prospectuses. Look for funds with consistent long-term track records and asses your level of risk using the questionnaire in the book. Then use the tables to split up the pie or split it up the way you feel most comfortable. Mix funds that have low correlations with each other. If you are looking for growth, weight your portfolio with domestic and overseas stock funds. Also put a small percentage in a gold fund and bond fund. This gives you an inflation hedge and an income cushion from bonds. Anchor your portfolio with a money fund. Higher-risk investors should keep about 20 percent in money funds. Low-risk investors should keep as much as 60 to 80 percent in money funds.

ENJOY INVESTING

You know more than anyone else what type of investment mix you feel comfortable with. Check your portfolio at least every three months. As your risk level or financial condition changes, change your asset-allocation mix. In addition, invest regularly. Pay yourself first and start a monthly savings plan. Use dollar cost averaging or rebalancing strategies to maximize your returns. Keep up with the financial news and learn to love investment decision making.

Sources of Information

MUTUAL-FUNDS NEWSLETTERS

"Donoghue's Moneyletter"
290 Eliot Street
Box 91004
Ashland, MA 01721

"Mutual Fund Forecaster"
The Institute of Econometric Research
3471 North Federal Highway
Fort Lauderdale, FL 33306

"The Hulbert Financial Digest"
316 Commerce Street
Alexandria, VA 22314

"The No Load Fund X"
DAL Investment Company
235 Montgomery Street
San Francisco, CA 94104

"The No Load Fund Investor"
P.O. Box 318
Irvington-on-Hudson, NY 10533

"The Mutual Fund Letter"
Investment Information Services, Inc.
205 West Wacker Drive
Chicago, IL 60606

"The Sector Funds Newsletter"
P.O. Box 1210
Escondido, CA 92025

"Switch Fund Advisory"
Schabacker Investment Management
8943 Shady Grove Court
Gaithersburg, MD 20877

"United Mutual Fund Selector"
United Business Services
210 Newbury Street
Boston, MA 02116

MUTUAL-FUNDS STATISTICAL SERVICES

CDA/Weisenberger
1355 Piccard Drive
Rockville, MD 20850

Donoghue's Mutual Funds Almanac
P.O. Box 540
Holliston, MA 01746

Handbook For No Load Investors
P.O. Box 283
Hastings-on-Hudson, NY 10706

Investment Company Data, Inc.
406 Merle Hay Tower
Des Moines, IA 50310

Johnson's Company Charts
246 Homewood Avenue
Buffalo, NY 14217

LaPorte Asset Allocation System
126 Petersburgh Rd.
Hackettstown, NJ 07840

Lipper Analytical Services
74 Trinity Place
New York, NY 10006

Mutual Fund Sourcebook
Morningstar, Inc.
53 West Jackson Street
Suite 352
Chicago, IL 60604

Wiesenberger Investment Company Service
210 South Street
Boston, MA 02110

MUTUAL-FUNDS BOOKS

Getting Started in Mutual Funds
By Alan Lavine
John Wiley & Sons
New York, NY

Dow Jones–Irwin Guide to Mutual Funds
By Rugg and Hale
Dow Jones–Irwin
Burr Ridge, IL

William E. Donoghue's No Load Mutual Fund Guide
By William E. Donoghue
Harper & Row
New York, NY

William E. Donoghue's Complete Money Market Guide
By William E. Donoghue
Harper & Row
New York, NY

Mutual Funds & Your Investment Portfolio
By Gerald W. Perritt
Investment Information Services
Chicago, IL

Mutual Fund Encyclopedia
By Gerald Perritt
Dearborn
Chicago, IL

Mutual Fund Fact Book
Investment Company Institute
Washington, DC

The Individual Investor's Guide
To No Load Mutual Funds
American Association of Individual Investors
Chicago, IL

Successful Investing In No Load Mutual Funds
By Alan Pope
John Wiley & Sons, Inc.
New York, NY

EMPLOYEE BENEFITS

Dow Jones–Irwin Guide to Personal Financial Planning
By William G. Droms and Fredrick Amling
Dow Jones–Irwin, Burr Ridge, IL

Fundamentals of Employees Benefit Programs
Employee Benefit Research Institute
Washington, DC

Your Life Insurance Options
By Alan Lavine
John Wiley & Sons
New York, NY

INDEX

A

AAA-rated bonds, 53, 103
Accredited Personal Financial
Planning Strategist (APFS),
222
Acorn Fund, 138
Acorn International Fund,
138
ADRs, 98–99
Aggressive-growth funds, 117
Aggressive-growth stock,
172–73
Aggressive portfolio, 134, 135
Akzo, 99
All-in-one funds, 148–54
All-weather portfolio, 15–16,
134, 136–37
American Eagle gold coins,
93, 97
American Depository Receipts
(ADRs), 98–99
Anheuser-Busch, 87
Archer, S. H., 14
Asia Pacific Fund, 98
Asset allocation, xiv
by age, 44–47
all-in-one funds, 148–54
arguments for, xv, 8, 84–86
comparison, 146–48
determining, 39–41, 44–47

performance evaluation,
143–56
portfolio, 131–32
Australian Nugget coin, 97
Automated teller machine
(ATM), 28

B

Babson Value Fund, 139
Balanced funds, 118
Balance sheet
company's, 70
personal, 23–24
Bank charges, 29
Bank time deposits, 53
Barron's, 80, 144, 146
Bartlett Basic Value Fund, 139
Baruch, Bernard, 5
Bass Limited, 99
B.A.T. Industries, 99
BB&K Diverse Fund, 153
Benham Group of Funds, 48
Benham, James, 48, 49
Benham Management, 226
Benham Treasury Note Fund,
139
Beta value, 10, 123
Blanchard Strategic Growth
Fund, 149, 154

Blue-chip stock values, 87,
88–89
Bonds and bond funds, 15, 40,
53–54, 119, 172–73
basics, 99
inflation, 106
selecting, 40–41, 122–32
yields, 53, 99–100
Bond ratings, 102–3
Boston Company, 226
Britannia coin, 97
British investments, 58, 99
Budgets, family, 25–27
Bull & Bear Group, 226
Bullion coins, 93, 97
Bull market, investing during,
170, 226
Business press, 80–81, 129,
144–45, 186, 228–29
Business Week, 80
Buy-and-hold strategy, 66,
67–68
and dollar cost averaging
compared, 168
market timing vs., 185–200

C

Cabbage Patch Kids, 62
Cafeteria 401(k) plans, 207
Calvert Asset Management,
226
Canadian Maple Leaf coins, 97
Capitalization, 71
Cash cows, 87, 91–92
Cash flow, 71–72
Cash management, 28–30
CDA/Wiesenberger, 123,
229
Certificates of Deposit (CDs),
29, 31, 120, 204
Certified Financial Planner
(CFP), 222

Certified Public Accountant
(CPA), 222
Charge cards, 29
Charles Schwab, 216
Chartered Financial
Consultant (ChFC), 222
Chartered Life Underwriter
(CLU), 222
Chua, Jess, 196
Clinton Administration, 49
Closed-end overseas stock
funds, 97, 98
Coleco, 62–63
Columbia Growth Fund, 152
Columbia Special Fund, 139
Commission on Money and
Credit, 105
Common stocks, 63, 115
Consolidation phase, 74, 76
Consumer Price Index (CPI),
105
Constant-dollar investment
strategy, 171–74
Constant-ratio investment
strategy, 171, 176–78
Constellation Growth Fund,
187
Corporate bonds, 115
Corporate growth, stages of,
72–75
Correlation, 14–16, 39, 42, 57
Crabble Huson Asset
Allocation Fund, 149
Credit risk, 31, 100, 101–2
Current ratio, 71
Current yield, 99–100

D

Daiwa, 99
Decay phase, 75
Defined-benefit retirement
plans, 207

Defined-contribution
retirement plans, 208
Deutsche Bank, 99
Direct-payroll-deposit
program, 29
Diversification mix, 42–43
Diversification risk, 31, 43
Dividend-paying nationally
traded companies, 92
Dividends, 87, 89–91
Dollar cost averaging, 159–68
"Donoghue's Moneyletter," 228
Donoghue's Mutual Funds
Almanac, 229
Dow Chemical, 74
Dow Jones Industrial Average,
118
*Dow Jones–Irwin Guide to
Mutual Funds,* 230
*Dow Jones–Irwin Guide to
Personal Financial
Planning,* 231

E

Earnings growth, 78–80
Earnings per share, 72, 78–79
Eastman Kodak, 118
Embryonic phase, 72–73
Employee benefits, information
sources, 231–32
Equity funds, 114–15, 124–25
Evaluating stocks, 63–66,
68–69, 70
Evans, J. L., 14
Evergreen Group, The, 226
Expense ratio, 123–24
Exxon, 74

F

Family budgets, 25–27
Fear, 196–97

Federal Home Loan Bank
Board (FHLBB), 119
Federal Home Loan Mortgage
Corporation (FHLMC),
119
Federally insured bank
accounts, 4
Federal National Mortgage
Association (FNMA), 119
Federal Reserve Bank of
St. Louis, 58
Fiat, 99
Fidelity Balanced Fund, 12
Fidelity Capital and Income
Fund, 178
Fidelity Capital Appreciation
Fund, 10
Fidelity Investments, 121, 216,
226
Fidelity Investments Asset
Manager Fund, 149,
151
Fidelity Investments Real
Estate Investment Fund,
52
Fidelity Magellan Fund, 118,
170, 191, 196
Fidelity Technology, 121
Financial goals, 21–22
Financial Industrial Income
Fund, 139–40
Financial news, effect on stock
market, 9
Financial planners, 28, 216,
221–22
*Financial Planning Under the
New Rules: An Investor's
Guide to the Tax Reform
Act of 1986,* 232
Financial press, 80–81, 129,
144–45, 186, 228–29
Financial Programs, 121, 226
Financial statements, 71–72

Financial strength of
companies, assessing,
70–72
Financial worth, determining,
23–24
First In First Out (FIFO), 91
Fixed-income risk, 100–101
"Folly of Stock Market Timing,
The," 194
Ford Motor Company, 118
Foreign bonds, 55, 57–58
Foreign investments, 15,
54–56, 97
Formula investing, 169–83
44 Wall Street Fund, 191
401(k) salary-reduction pension
plans, 204, 205–7
Founders Discovery Fund, 140
France Fund, 98
Franklin Income Fund, 119
French investments, 58
Fuji Film, 99
*Fundamentals of Employee
Benefit Programs,* 231
Fund Exchange, 152
Fund profiles, 138–42

G

General Motors, 74, 118
German investments, 58
Germany Fund, 98
Gold, 49, 50, 93–97
Government bonds, 115
Government National
Mortgage Association
(GNMA), 119
Government securities, 119–20
Graham, Benjamin, 193
Great Depression, 3
Growth and income funds,
118

Growth-and-income portfolio,
131, 134, 135
Growth funds, 117–18
Growth portfolio, 130–31
Growth rates, 77
Growth stocks
prices, 76–81
recommendations, 82–83
selecting, 72

H

*Handbook for No-Load Fund
Investors, The,* 111, 229
Hedging, 14–15
Helvetica Fund, 98
Hitachi, 99
Home equity loan, 30
"Hulbert Financial Digest,"
186, 228
Hulbert, Mark, 196
Hutzler, Harry, 187

I

Ibbotson Associates of Chicago,
58, 69, 115
Income based on life
expectancy, 203–4
Income funds, 119
Income portfolio, 131, 134,
135–36
Income statement, 70
*Individual Investor's Guide to
No Load Mutual Funds,
The,* 231
Individual Retirement
Accounts (IRAs), 93,
204–5
Individual securities, 61–108
Industrial life cycle, 75

Inflation, 9, 32, 49, 104–6
Insider trading, 97
Institute of Certified Financial
    Planning, 222
Institutional investors, 62
*Intelligent Investor and
    Security Analysis, The,* 193
Interest rate risk, 31, 100–101
Interest rates
  and bond prices, 4, 9, 53
  foreign, 58
  short-term, 49
Interest-rate timing, 40
Intermediate goals, 23
International Association for
    Financial Planning, 28,
    222
Investment Company Data,
    Inc., 230
Investment Company Institute,
    4
Investment Horizons, 81
Investment Information
    Services, 81
Investment mix, 34, 36–37,
    41–42, 58
Investment performance,
    evaluating, 143–56
Investment profile, 36
Investment pyramid, 34, 35
Investment risk(s), xiii–xiv, 33
Investments, selecting, 34,
    68–108
IRAs, 93, 204–5
Italian investments, 98, 99
Italy Fund, 98
Ivy Growth Funds, 226

J

Jack White and Company, 216
Jacobs, Sheldon, 111, 166
Janus Fund, 152

Japanese investments, 58,
    99
Jeffrey Company, The, 194
Jeffrey, Robert H., 194
Jones & Babson, 226
Journal of Finance, 14
Junk bonds, 31, 199

K

Korea Fund, 98

L

Laddered portfolio, 47
LaPorte Asset Allocation
    System, 135, 230
Last In Last Out (LILO), 91
Lexington Funds, 226
Lexington Gold Fund, 140
Life expectancy, 203–4
Life insurance, 208–14
Limited partnerships, 50–51
Lindner Fund, 140
Lipper Analytical Services,
    32, 53, 94, 114, 144–45,
    230
Lipper, Michael, 32
Liquidity, and mutual funds,
    116
Load mutual funds, 110–11
Long-term approach to
    investing, 62–64
Long-term gains, 69
Long-term goals, 23
Lost opportunity, 31
Louis, Joe, 21
Low cost mutual funds, 116

M

Margin of error, 17, 123
Market risk, 8–9

Market timing, 31, 185–200
Maturity phase, 74–75
Maximum loss periods, 68
Merck, 118
Merriman Investment Trust, 152
Merriman, Paul, 152
Meyer, Andre, 22
MIMLIC Asset Allocation Fund, 152
Mining stocks, selecting, 95–96; *See also* Gold
Model mutual-funds portfolios, 133–42
Moderately aggressive portfolio, 134, 135
Money funds, 41, 52, 172–73, 179–80
Money-market funds, 29, 120
Moody's, 102
Morgan Stanley & Co., 56
Morningstar Mutual Funds, 127
Mutual Fund Fact Book, 231
"Mutual Fund Forecaster," 228
"Mutual Fund Letter, The," 229
Mutual funds, 50, 109–32
    advantages of, 110, 114–15, 116–17
    appropriate number to hold, 129–30
    averages by group, 150
    best managed, 126, 128
    changes in, 215–23
    evaluating performance, 52, 113, 125–29, 143–56
    five-year returns, 190
    long-term performance, 115–17
    model portfolios, 133–42
    no-load vs. load, 110–11, 112
    profiles, 138–42
    strategies, 130–32
    types, 117–22

Mutual funds books, 230–31
Mutual funds newsletters, 228–29
Mutual Fund Sourcebook, 123, 145, 230
"Mutual Fund Specialist," 228
Mutual funds statistical services, 229–30
Mutual Funds & Your Investment Profile, 231

N

National Partnership Exchange, 50
Net asset value (NAV), calculating, 111
Netherlands, investments, 58, 99
Net-profit margin, 71
Neuberger & Berman, 226
Newspaper quotations, reading, 113
Nicholas Fund, 152
Nissan Motor Co., 99
"No Load Fund Investor, The," 166, 229
"No Load Fund X, The," 228
No Load Investor, 166
No-Load Mutual Fund Council, 142
No-load mutual funds, 29, 110–14
Nonmarket risk, 12
No Transaction Fee (NTF) mutual funds, 216–17

O

Operating-profit margin, 71
Overseas investments, 54–56, 97

Overseas mutual funds, 56–57,
98, 121

P

Paine Webber Asset Allocation
Fund, 151
Par value, 100
Pension plans, traditional, 207
Performance evaluation,
143–56
Permanent portfolio, 149, 154
Personal level of risk, xv,
21–37, 43–44, 181–83
Pfizer, 74
Phillip Morris, 74, 87
Portfolio turnover rate, 124
PRA Real Estate Securities, 52
Precious metals, 15, 49, 50, 93,
121–22
Precious metals mutual funds,
121–22
Price swings, 115–17
Price-to-earnings multiples, 78,
80, 87
Price-to-earnings ratio (p/e), 70
Price volatility, 10–12, 34
Professional management of
mutual funds, 114
Profit-sharing plans, 206–7
Public utilities, 62
Purchasing-power risk, 40

Q

Quisenberry, Dan, 159

R

Real Estate Investment Trusts
(REITs), 50, 51–52
Real estate tax, 30
Rebalancing, 178–83

Reinvesting dividends, 90–91
Retirement savings plans,
201–14
Return on equity, 71, 87
Risk level, personal, xv, 21–37,
43–44, 181–83
Risk test, 32–33
Risk versus return, 16–20, 32
Ritter, Lawrence, 49
Rogers, Will, 169

S

Safeco Income Fund, 140–41,
152, 226
Salary-reduction plans, 205–6
Salomon Brothers Center for
the Study of Financial
Research, 50, 57
Salomon Brothers Corporate
Bond Index, 144, 177, 192
Scandinavian Fund, 98
Scudder Group of Mutual
Funds, 220
Scudder Horizon Plan, 220
Scudder International Fund,
178
Scudder New Asia Fund, 98
Sector funds, 121–22
"Sector Funds Newsletter,
The," 229
Self-employed Keogh plans, 208
Senior citizens, 46–47
SEP plans, 208
Sharp Corporation, 99
Short-term goals, 23
Short term swings, 69
Simplified Employee Pension
(SEP), 208
Single-premium life insurance,
211
Sources and Uses of Funds
statement, 70–71

Spending cuts, 26, 27–28
Stand-alone retirement plans, 207
Standard and Poor's, 69, 102
Standard and Poor's Bond and Stock Guides, 124, 145
Standard and Poor's Stock Guide, 145
Standard and Poor's 500 (S&P 500), 7, 10, 64, 65, 70, 90, 107, 118, 144, 177
Standard deviation; *See* Margin of error
Start-up companies, characteristics of, 73
Stein Roe & Farnham, 226
Stock and bond fund trades, 172–73
Stock market crash, October 1987, xiii, 3–4, 5, 166
Stock market history, 6, 198–200
Stock selection, 63, 68–108
Stocks
    balanced portfolio of, 85–86
    evaluating performance, 63–66, 144–46
    inflation and, 104–5, 106–8
Stocks vs. Treasury bills, 65, 66
Strong Total Return Fund, 118
Successful Investing in No Load Mutual Funds, 231
"Switch Fund Advisory," 229
Switzerland, 58
Systematic investment or withdrawal, and mutual funds, 116–17

T

"Tactical-asset-allocation," 151
Taiwan Fund, 98

Tax-deferred growth, 202
Tax Reform Act of 1986, 206, 207
Tax strategies, 29–30
Templeton Real Estate Securities, 52
Term insurance, 209
Thrift plans, 206
Time, importance of, 44
Total return funds, 118–19
Treasury bills, 52–53, 65, 66, 103, 189; *See also* U. S. Treasury securities
Treasury bonds, 40, 53–54, 63, 103–4
Treasury notes, 103
T. Rowe Price Equity Income Fund, 141
T. Rowe Price International Bond Fund, 141
T. Rowe Price investment company, 186, 226
Twain, Mark, 3
20th Century Growth Fund, 10, 11
Twentieth Century Investors, 226

U

Undervalued stocks, 62
United Kingdom, investments, 58, 99
"United Mutual Fund Selector," 229
United Services Advisors, 226–27
United Services Gold Fund, 178
Universal life insurance, 210
Urich, Thomas, 49
USAA Cornerstone Fund, 149, 153

USAA Investment
 Management, 227
U.S. bond market vs.
 international bond
 market, 55
U.S. stocks vs. foreign stocks,
 54
U.S. Treasury securities, 4, 15,
 52–53, 65, 103–4, 115
Utilities, 62

V

Value-added gain, 144
Value Line, Inc., 227
Value Line Investment Survey,
 10, 70, 87, 98, 124
Value Line Leveraged Growth
 Fund, 117
Vanguard, 121
Vanguard Asset Allocation
 Fund, 149, 151
Vanguard Group of Funds, 220,
 227
Vanguard Index 500 Fund,
 41, 162, 178
Vanguard Short-Term Bond
 Fund Corporate, 141
Vanguard Small Capitalization
 Stock Fund, 141

Vanguard Variable Annuity
 Plan, 220–21
Vanguard World-U.S. Growth
 Fund, 142
Variable annuities, 217–21
Variable life insurance, 210–11
Volkswagen, 99

W

Wagner, Ralph, 138
Wall Street Journal, 62, 80
Whole life insurance, 210
*Wiesenberger's Investment
 Company Service,* 145,
 230
*William E. Donoghue's
 Complete Money Market
 Guide, 230*
*William E. Donoghue's
 No Load Mutual Fund
 Guide, 230*
Woodward, Richard, 196
World Gold Council, 96

Y

Yield curve, 48–49
Yield to maturity, 100

Dr. Gerald Perritt's

the Mutual Fund Letter

Wealth-Building Strategies for the Astute Investor

"One of America's Most Widely Read Mutual Fund Advisory Newsletters"

Edited by Dr. Gerald Perritt and published since 1983.

- Investment Outlook & Strategy
- Investment Ideas and Portfolio Management Strategies
- Model Portfolios for Five Investment Objectives
- Buy-Hold-Sell Advice for Specific Funds
- Fund Family Reports
- and *Much More!*

Heard Through the Grapevine...

"If you're the type to follow a newsletter's advice to a T, then you might try The Mutual Fund Letter...among the top-ranked fund letters for the past three years."

—USA Today

"A lot of stuff packed in here."

—Kiplinger's Changing Times

"Gerald W. Perritt has been crusading for better-informed investing for more than a decade—first as a college professor, then as director of a nonprofit group, and now as newsletter publisher and author of books on investing."

—St. Petersburg Times

Call today for a free sample of the latest issue!
1-800-326-6941